At last:
A Smarter Way to Market
and Grow a Professional Practice

Also by Ned Steele:

102 Publicity Tips to Grow a Business or Practice

Available at Amazon.com

Attract New Prospects,
Get More Clients!

AWAKEN THE MARKETER IN YOU

How to Accelerate the Growth
of Your Professional Practice

NED STEELE

Andover, Minnesota

ISBN 13: 978-1-931945-77-6
ISBN 10: 1-931945-77-2

Library of Congress Catalog Number: 2007929680

Printed in the United States of America
First Printing: June 2007
11 10 09 08 07   5 4 3 2 1

Cover design by George Foster

 Expert Publishing, Inc.
14314 Thrush Street NW,
Andover, MN 55304-3330

Andover, 1-877-755-4966
Minnesota www.expertpublishinginc.com

For more information:
Media*Impact*
New York, NY
info@MediaImpact.biz
www.MediaImpact.biz
This book is available at Amazon.com and at www.MediaImpact.biz.
For group and bulk purchases, special rates are available.
Please contact info@MediaImpact.biz.

To all the independent professionals, professional practices, entrepreneurs, and organizations that are ready to take the next step—the one that will start them on a new path to smarter business development and better outcomes.

CONTENTS

Foreword *by Mark LeBlanc* / *vii*

Introduction / *1*

WAKE UP OR DIE / *7*

YES, YOU CAN / *17*

THE THREE TRAPS THAT CAN DOOM YOUR MARKETING / *23*

BE THE FLAME / *33*

A SMARTER, BETTER WAY: USING THE mPOWER SYSTEM / *41*

WHAT IF YOUR PROSPECTS ACTUALLY LISTENED TO YOU? / 53

LET'S FINALLY *DO* SOMETHING / 63

14 SIMPLE STRATEGIES TO ATTRACT PROSPECTS / 73

YOU'RE NOT SPAM / 83

HAVING A WEB SITE IS NOT AN INTERNET STRATEGY / 89

THE BEST WAY TO GET PUBLICITY: DATE A CELEBRITY.
HERE'S THE SECOND BEST WAY / 105

BUILD AND SUSTAIN MOMENTUM / 117

APPENDIX:
The mPOWER Checklist: 25 Things to do Now / 121

POSTSCRIPT: Yes, You Will / 125

Want to Learn More? / 126

FOREWORD

When it comes to marketing a professional practice, few people truly understand how to help position you as an expert resource for your prospects and help you attract clients.

Ned Steele is one of the very few and is uniquely qualified to write and speak on the subject of marketing a service practice. Ned is a consummate professional. His street-smart expertise, and an amazing collection of personal and professional experiences, have shaped his thinking and enhanced his mix of strategies and tactics for making something happen in your business.

His expertise, developed by working with both business celebrities and countless small- and mid-sized professional service firms, has contributed to his colorful insights and depth of content.

Many books contain marketing theory and are an exercise in reading that, quite frankly, is boring. Ned captures your attention from the first few pages and then moves quickly into what you need to know, what you need to do, and most important, how you need to think every day about marketing your business.

Read this book. Then read it again. Then read it again, and make notes. Then use the book and your notes to create an action plan that will get you more visibility, make you a more credible professional, and develop more business.

The pie is huge, and it's yours for the taking. In these times of change, however, it is critical for you to think beyond the belief that the quality of your services alone is enough to build your business. That was the "old school" way of doing business. The new way of doing business is contained in this book, and it works—if you do!

—Mark LeBlanc
Author of *Growing Your Business!*
2007-2008 President of the National Speakers Association

INTRODUCTION

Once upon a time, I was a big-city newspaper reporter. I wrote about fires, murders, excruciatingly boring government meetings, and the occasional horrific disaster. I even got to pretend-cover a few wars. (I would sit at my computer terminal in the newsroom, combining and rewriting wire-service dispatches from distant combat zones; the editors would put my byline on top and print them.)

It was all a heck of a lot of fun. You got to poke holes in the inflated egos of pompous politicians and ego-mad celebrities all day, and then go to cool press parties at night. But the best part was this: you got to hang up the phone on anybody who annoyed you unnecessarily, without having to worry about being polite. Most of the time, you did this to public-relations people who couldn't do their job properly.

Then the time came, as it does for many reporters, to grow up and find a real job. Eventually, I became one of those public-relations people I used to hang up on.

Clients would inevitably implore me to approach my former colleagues with exactly the kind of story pitch that would have driven me, in my reporter days, to hang up instantly with no remorse. Usually, the story my clients wanted me to place in the news media was some variation of this: "Six Reasons Why I Am Great and Important."

It didn't take much to realize that if I wouldn't have touched such a story when I was a reporter, no other credible journalist would do it either. Not even if they owed me a favor. Not even when the clients really *were* great and important. (Because when they were, the media would *want* to do the story and wouldn't wait for a PR agent's call.)

I knew I had to find another way to get the result I wanted.

That realization changed my career forever. I saw that to succeed, I would have to create a different approach—one that somehow made the story newsworthy, compelling, of interest to a larger audience. It had to meet the needs of the reporter I was pitching. It couldn't be all about the client; yet it still had to portray the client strongly and positively. With a little ingenuity and persistence, I usually found a way to achieve this—as most capable PR people do.

Some years later, I had branched out. I was now providing a wider array of marketing services. But I still encountered the same situation: clients would fixate in their marketing materials on telling people why they were great. Then they'd wonder why their slick new brochures, mailers, and ads didn't drive in a stampede of new business. Again, I had to remind them: "The world doesn't care when it's about *you*. They only pay attention when it's about *them*."

But how to be about *them* when ultimately, especially if you are a small or mid-sized professional practice, firm, or organization—the people I wrote this book for—it *is* about you? How do you convince your prospects that you, and not the competitor firm across town, are the one to hire? There has to be a way, I thought: a better way to market and grow a talented yet modestly-sized financial planning, law, medical, accounting, insurance, real estate, consulting firm, or any other entrepreneurial practice or organization.

There *is* a better, smarter way. This book will show it to you.

Do you remember that puzzle you'd do as a school kid: "What's Wrong With This Picture?" You'd stare at the intricate drawing on the page for a long time, unable to find anything amiss. Finally you'd spot it: the monkey in the tree had two tails. Or that nicely-dressed woman in the restaurant was cutting her steak with a spoon. Well, there's an adult version of this game, and you may have played it.

You look long and hard at the jumbled picture that is your business or your livelihood, and you know in your gut that something is not quite right. You're doing okay, but you're not yet soaring. Yet everything in the picture seems as it should be.

You've earned all the degrees and credentials your field requires.

You've paid your dues, working diligently for a number of years, perhaps at first with a large, highly-respected organization before striking out in your own venture.

You've got clients—maybe even lots of them—and they hold you in high regard. As they should–you do good work for them.

You make sure to get to a few networking events a year. You never go anywhere without a good supply of business cards, and rarely do you pass up an opportunity to seek out a referral. Your web site is up and running; you even churn out a marketing piece or two yearly.

Still, the pipeline of prospects—your next new clients—isn't as full as it should be. So, what's missing from the picture?

This book will tell you. If the above description even remotely fits you or your business, you're the person I wrote this book for.

I walked past a bar some time ago, and it caught my eye like few bars ever have. We were in a smallish airport terminal building, just a handful of gates. Why did this bar capture my attention at 11:00 in the morning? Not for any unsavory reason. But it did take me a moment to realize what made it stand out.

The exterior was handsome, dark wood paneling—and nothing else. Not a sign, logo, or identifier. It didn't have a name. It didn't have an identity.

It didn't need one. If you were waiting for a plane and wanted a beer, it was where you went. It was the only watering hole in the terminal.

The guy who owns that bar is the only person I can think of who doesn't need to market his business and communicate with his prospects. This book is for everyone else.

The business that doesn't have to worry about the ideas in this book

Have you ever had this odd experience while glancing over the community bulletin board at the laundromat or the supermarket? You know the one: Scrawled on an index card up near the top of the board, some desperate parent is crying out for a good babysitter. And neatly printed down on the lower left is someone in the same neighborhood, advertising their services as... a babysitter. *Gosh,* you think, *if only one of them would walk by here right now—both their problems would be solved!* You toy for a moment with the idea of calling one or the other and telling them they've got a match. But of course you never do.

And, if you're like me, you may pause a moment to contemplate the parallels between their plight and that of every other professional and would-be client in the marketplace. Perhaps the situation even reminds you of your own situation.

Isn't business just like that, you think. *So many worthy, talented professionals out there, and so many people in need of their services.*

Yet professionals constantly struggle to attract and win new clients, while those potential new clients are often equally frustrated.

They don't know where to turn, whom to ask. Maybe they get a referral from someone; sometimes it all works out. The whole process seems so hit-and-miss. *Why,* you wonder, *can't they just find each other more easily?*

And you daydream: *wouldn't it be perfect if some giant unseen hand in the marketplace could bring professional and client together as effortlessly as it would be to just tape those two cards on the bulletin board right next to each other?*

As we know, it's not that simple in the real world. But it's not so far off. Nobody can make new clients fall into your lap magically. But I believe you *can* learn a new way of thinking and acting that will have almost the same effect. It's a mindset and a system that sets forces in motion to attract new clients and draw prospects into your life who you don't even know yet. It's a pretty simple, down-to-earth, step-by-step approach. And while it's so common-sense that anybody can do it, the difference it makes *can* be magical to your business.

I learned another life-changing lesson as a reporter. Sometimes you could work and work at a story about something that interested you greatly. You'd spend hours digging deep and then honing it to what felt like perfection.

But if they thought your topic wasn't as intriguing or relevant to the readership, the editors would bury it in the back of the paper. And no one (except maybe your mother) would notice it, not even your colleagues.

And then, when you got assigned to a really big story, one the whole town was talking about, you'd be a celebrity in the newsroom for the day. You landed on Page One, perhaps. Slaps on the back on the elevator, high-fives in the cafeteria, and all that. The quality of your writing and reporting might even have been just so-so this time. But it didn't matter. You got to enjoy your turn as Mr. or Ms. Big Shot.

Lesson learned: in any kind of communication (which is what marketing is), not only is it not about *you,* it's also not necessarily about what interests you most, or what you do best. Once again, it's about what interests *them*—the marketplace. And doing even an adequate, competent job of it, as long as you're connecting with what the marketplace wants and needs, will bring you success.

I'm not going to champion mediocrity and rail against excellence in these pages—far from it. But I do want you to know that you don't need to be the most credentialed, knowledgeable, or experienced practitioner, and you certainly don't have to be the most skillful writer or marketer, to succeed at the principles in this book. If you are good enough to have clients who hire you, you can do anything I discuss in here.

This book is interactive. Don't be surprised if you come to a page where I ask you to put your reading down for a moment and turn briefly to my web site or some other resource for additional enrichment. At times I will encourage you to send me your own field observations (or questions) about some phenomenon or topic I'm discussing. I want to know what you're thinking and seeing as you do business. I really do. Not merely because I'm curious, but because I may learn something that I can share with others. We learn from each other. The radio traffic reporter in my town (which happens to be New York City) constantly gives out his toll-free number over the air and urges drivers to call in with word of any traffic jams they encounter. He embodies my model for marketing. You don't hold back your information in selfish fear that you might be giving away the store or helping the competition. Your audience is traveling on another road somewhere else. You just do it for the benefit of those who are traveling a little behind you.

Before you turn to chapter 1, please promise yourself that you'll believe this one thing: Believe that you *can* market and grow your business. Even if marketing is the last thing you want to do; even if at this moment you're sure you can't.

And believe this, too: Half of you who read this book are going to go one better than the ideas suggested in here and come up with spectacular new ways to succeed. When you do, I hope you'll share them with me.

1
WAKE UP OR DIE

I"It feels like going to the dentist."

Many professionals in small or mid-size practices—whether accounting, financial planning, law, medicine, real estate, or any other—have told me that's how it feels when the time comes to do something about marketing their business.

This is the secret thought bouncing around their skulls, where no one can see it:

I know I have to do this, but do I really have to do it? Isn't there some other way to get business?

Why *do* so many professionals dislike getting involved with what they often think of as "that marketing stuff?" Because it doesn't play to their strengths or aptitudes. They're not comfortable doing it—whether "doing it" consists of actually creating a marketing piece themselves, or simply overseeing, signing off on, and paying for work created by a an outside expert. In some fields—notably medicine and law—self-promotion is viewed ambiguously and even negatively as a tricky affair with ethical issues attached, requiring careful regulation. Maybe it's also a left brain-right brain thing. I don't know. All I know is that they feel discomfort. After all, if they had truly enjoyed "that marketing stuff," they probably would have studied it in school, or gone on to careers in it. But instead, they are practicing law, or medicine, or financial planning—and with good reason: they are good at it, and the profession they chose probably suits their aptitude and temperament.

I understand this feeling. It's how *I* feel when I have to get my taxes done, or work on the financial books, or fill out long, complicated forms: *I know I have to do this, but do I* really *have to do it?*

Here are some of the ways it comes out sounding when people in professional practices get in touch—often subconsciously—with their inner feelings about marketing I have heard all of these lines over the years:

"I hate doing this marketing stuff."

"What's the point? We can't outspend the big guys."

"This stuff doesn't work. I tried it before."

"I don't need marketing... I get my business from word of mouth."

"I can't understand why we don't stand out in the marketplace."

"We do such good work. If only the market knew about us…"

"Our best marketing tool is me. I just have to get out there and meet more people."

"I just leave it all to our marketing person. She's supposed to be the expert."

"I wish I could afford a marketing person."

"Our marketing person just doesn't get what we're all about."

"We're great at reacting to opportunities, but we never seem to create any."

Do any of those sound familiar?

If this isn't you, if you are one of those who like marketing, and are happy with your results, stop reading here. You don't need to find a whole new perspective. But if you're among the other 97 percent of the professional services population, please read on.

By age eight or so, most of us accept that yes, we do have to visit the dentist occasionally. Similarly, most professionals at some point recognize that marketing is something they need to do, buy, or oversee, even if they'd rather be devoting full energy to serving clients. (Just as I accept that I must sit down with my accountant, who's really an extremely nice guy, several times a year.) So they plunge in and do *something* in the hope it will stir up some new business.

But, more often than not, they do it from a weakened, impaired state. They lack one or more of the critical ingredients for success: enthusiasm, aptitude, or confidence. They feel like the proverbial fish out of water, and they flounder and flop around just like one of them. Even if they are fortunate enough to afford a marketing agency or staff person, they feel unqualified or unable to evaluate their recommendations and make the right decisions.

Here's a surprise for you: this book is *not* going to teach you how to be better, more comfortable, or smarter about marketing—at least not marketing in the standard sense. Rather, this book's central underlying premise is:

THERE'S A GOOD REASON WHY YOU'VE ALWAYS SECRETLY FELT UNEASY AND UNCOMFORTABLE ABOUT MARKETING YOUR FIRM.

The Six Reasons Why 90 Percent Of Professional Services' Marketing Is Doomed To Fail

OK, this is my bold assertion: 90 percent of traditional, by-the-textbook marketing for professional services doesn't work. It doesn't bring enough new business in the door to justify its cost in time, energy, and dollars. Especially for smaller firms or practices.

Which is the 10 percent that *does* work? I wish I knew. Nobody does, despite what you may hear. If I did, I'd be a genius.

Truth is, it's rarely the same 10 percent. Different strategies, different media succeed at different times for different reasons. So, rather than try to scope out the un-knowable, let's look at how you can improve the odds. To do that, you need to understand *why* 90 percent of traditional practice marketing doesn't work. Here are the six reasons:

1. **Marketing is a tough game.** This goes for everyone, including the corporate giants and all the supposed experts. Marketing is imprecise, often based on subjective factors, despite the field's best efforts to look and sound like a science. Trust me on this: no one really knows for sure what's going to work. If you doubt this, glance over the news stories about the advertising industry for the next few weeks. Day after day, you'll see reports of new ad campaigns being launched, of companies trying new strategies, often using new, high-tech media. The announcements are always accompanied by confident predictions that this time the marketer has hit upon something that really works. But the reason they're launching all these new campaigns is that the last one didn't work. And you know what? The people who created that last campaign were just as smart, just as experienced, and just as creative as the ones who dreamed up the new one. In fact, they are often the same people! If you ever want to waste time enjoyably, surf the Internet and try to track how many different ad campaigns and slogans the likes of Burger King or Coca-Cola have rolled out over the years. Now if the big behemoths, with their unlimited access to talent, can't hit on a winning formula—what chance do we little folks have of getting it right?

2. **Marketing a professional practice is even harder.** Virtually all of the textbook knowledge, and most of the resident expertise in business schools and in the marketing profession, are centered around marketing consumer products. These products are real, tangible, and available for sale in the nearest mall or corner store. It's comparatively easy for the buyer to examine and compare features, pros and cons, price, and value. But a professional service is the exact opposite. It's intangible, sub-

jective, personal, and hard to consistently define value. Author Harry Beckwith calls this Selling the Invisible. (A good book to read, by the way.) A professional service is not an item you buy off the shelf, not an impulse purchase, not something where you can pull out a commonly agreed-on yardstick to measure and compare two competitors. Making things worse, many of us fail to understand what we are selling. We think the client is buying our brains and our skills. She's not. What we are selling is a relationship of trust in which we deploy those skills. Go try marketing that concept with strategies and tactics originally invented to sell potato chips. You'll end up deader than an Oldsmobile.

3. **We are small businesses in a cluttered world.** The average American is exposed to thousands–yes thousands–of ad or marketing messages a day. The clutter is pervasive, and it is being driven by the largest corporations on earth. CBS launched a new TV season by laser-engraving the names of its shows on millions of eggs sold at the supermarket. Advertisers are slapping their messages on buildings, city sidewalks, restroom stalls–even on people. They're embedding them, with Hollywood's cheery cooperation, in movies and television shows. The experts even have a name for it: "ad creep."

What Do You Think?

Send me the most intrusive or unexpected place you've seen an ad lately. I'll publish the best submissions in my monthly e-newsletter and on my web site. Send to info@Mediaimpact.biz. Some of my recent "favorites":

- [ ] A forty-acre Kansas cornfield (CBS)
- [ ] On the sidewalk outside my office (Nivea)
- [ ] On a sculpture in an art gallery (Kao Corp.)
- [ ] Disguised as a fake for-sale ad in the classifieds (Hasbro)

Send in yours, and I'll publish it.

All this reminds me of when I'd pick up my son's Little League team after the game in my minivan. Doors would fly open on all sides, and I'd be barraged with little voices shouting excitedly from every direction as the kids piled in. Who would I hear amid all that babble? Whichever voice was loudest or most persistent. Well, the corporate parallel to the loudest and most persistent nine-year-old is the company that spends the most to put its name everywhere. Is that you? I didn't think so. It's not me either. We'll have to find another way if we want to be noticed, much less listened to. Don't try and hack your way through the jungle with a pocketknife because you can't afford a machete. Few of us have the resources to slash our way through the clutter.

Egg ads? Egads!
If advertising is everywhere these days,
how can we stand out?

4. **We're talking about the wrong people.** We tend to talk way too much in our marketing and promotion materials about how we are great/indispensable/ideally qualified/a perfect fit… and I could go on. This is a major disconnect, and a central theme of this book. The market does not care about us. It cares only about itself. They care about themselves. Why are we talking about us? What Madison Avenue does so well is to create messages and images that connect viscerally to our inner wants, needs, and emotions. Since it takes megabucks to do this well (putting aside the larger question of whether it's right to do it), that pretty much rules out all us non mega-sized businesses. There are no shortcuts. If you cannot afford the millions it takes to subtly and pervasively channel your prospects' emotions, you need to find a better, affordable way to focus on their needs.

5. **We all look the same.** It's astonishing how similar professional practices' marketing materials look. It's as if there are two templates for each profession on the shelf in Staples, and everybody picks up one or the other and strolls happily to the register. We all seem to be stuck on an image in our minds of what it's supposed to look like. How are we going to stand out in the marketplace when the effect of our marketing piece is to make us not stand out? Even worse is the way in which we look the same: many of us are trying, consciously or subconsciously, to mimic the look of the giant firms. We seem to be thinking (and I have heard clients voice this thought explicitly): "We'll show the market we're as good as the big firms. We'll put out some pieces that look like theirs." I could go on all day about the perils of trying to look or act like something you're not. Enough said for now. If you want a sure-fire route to failure, try to look like the big guys.

6. **We're just not comfortable enough.** As I said earlier, most folks in the professional services are, obviously, not marketing people. So they're ill at ease, at best, when it comes to marketing. Even if they outsource to a professional, they still have to find that marketing professional or firm, assess their capabilities

and how well they fit, and then oversee, improve, and approve the project. Even this is often anguishing: how do you, an accountant, lawyer, or physician, assess what's good and right for you? One of my favorite clients, one of the smartest people I know, asked his brochure writer to pop out a press release. He was astounded when it fizzled: Isn't a writer a writer? The answer, as anyone in the writing or marketing field knows, is no—writers specialize. My client simply had no clue from the get-go. The point: when you lack knowledge, expertise, experience, comfort, and grounding in an endeavor, the results are not likely to soar—even if you outsource. Two bad ways to build a house if you're not a carpenter: 1) pick up the hammer yourself; 2) tell a builder, "Just make me something I'll like."

Want an eight-second test of whether your current marketing materials are any good?

Take them off your shelf, or print them out, and set them aside for a day or two. Then, find a quiet moment away from your office, sit down and look at them with fresh eyes. Be objective—and brutally honest. Ask yourself: "IF I GOT THIS IN THE MAIL, WOULD I READ IT?"

So Let's Recap:

Let's quit talking about ourselves so much.

Let's quit looking like each other, which we are inadvertently doing in the name of differentiating our businesses.

Let's quit blowing the budget on "marketing stuff" we don't understand or can't pass judgment on comfortably.

Let's quit hoping the so-called experts will "get it right" for us.

Let's quit fooling ourselves that one attractive-looking, well-written marketing piece is going to drive business development for us.

Instead, let's start to focus on:

- Talking to and about the audience we're trying to reach.
- Identifying, understanding, communicating, and marketing our own uniqueness and strengths in a way that relates to the marketplace's needs and interests.
- Building relationships with prospects that lead to more sales and with referral sources that lead to more referrals.

In short, I am asking you to awaken the marketer in you—even if you think it's not in there, even if marketing and promotion work feels truly painful, or difficult, or confusing, or just not enjoyable. Because if you don't, in the end you're *really* going to be unhappy.

Want to Know More?

To see some of the ridiculous and intrusive places ads have popped up recently, visit the Ad-Creep Gallery on my web site. Click on www. MediaImpact.biz/resources/adcreep. But beware—this isn't for the faint of heart.

YES, YOU CAN

If you have attended elementary school in the past thirty years, or parented a child who did, you have surely heard plenty of the "everyone is special" lingo.

Well, what if it turned out to be true?

For years, I looked somewhat skeptically at the self-esteem mindset behind the "we're all special" bandwagon. Surely, I thought, plenty of kids must be average—or worse. Why deceive them or give them false encouragement, I wondered.

Then one day, I looked around at the adults we had become. And, lo and behold, we *were* all special.

Some of us were writers, some engineers. Some were accountants, shop clerks, technicians, heavy machinery salespeople, toll collectors, tax lawyers, police officers, financial planners, wedding planners, bakers, and nonprofit executives.

Maybe not all of us were tops in our game, at the pinnacle of our chosen profession. But in twenty-five years of working with business leaders and ordinary business folk, I have become convinced of this: each of us *does* possess our own distinct specialness, our own uniqueness.

We are all uniquely a blend of talents and personality that the marketplace finds appealing enough to keep us in business and working.

Whether we are in professional services, or entrepreneurs, or running an organization, we all have a special expertise with which we serve the marketplace. Most likely, we have honed, developed, and sharpened it over the years. After all this time, we are good at what we do.

And if we are fortunate, we have embraced this strength—and so we like what we do. We feel complete, engaged, fulfilled when we are doing it. Our expertise, during that part of the day when we work, becomes our center. It is the place where we dwell psychically—where we define ourselves and find self-fulfillment, professionally.

I know that I am in that place when I am writing, researching, updating my flagship speaking program, or actually delivering it on stage.

I know I am *not* in that place when I have to work on the bookkeeping or perform a statistical analysis of *anything*.

Things don't change that much from high school, it turns out. Can you remember looking for any diversion or excuse to put off the homework from the classes you hated? But for that one subject or teacher you loved, you'd sink deeply for hours, almost unaware, into an extended and complicated project.

In that state, whether you're a carpenter crafting an exquisite cabinet or a high-powered attorney orating in the courtroom, you're almost oblivious to the passage of time or the world around you. This past summer I had a repairman come in to fix my air-conditioner. I just wanted to get back quickly to my writing and wasn't interested in idle chatter. This guy was unlikely to share a passion for any topic that interested me, anyway. But just get him started on the subject of heating and cooling—as I unintentionally did—and a gleam would appear in his eye. He could go on all day on the myriad issues relating to ventilation.

Athletes call this being in "the Zone." Whatever our profession, it's the state where we're fully engaged doing what we do and love. It's not only where we make our money, but where we are at our best. It's where—dare I say it—we are *happy*.

It's where, hopefully, we spend a fair amount of our time when we're at work serving our clients or customers.

So tell me, then: why do so many of us voluntarily put ourselves in *some other place* when the time comes to market and build our business?

But that's what a lot of us do, isn't it?

I think you know what I mean. When we need to do some marketing, or business development, or promotion work to attract new clients, immediately we start thinking of it as something unfamiliar, different, uncomfortable. Perhaps even alien. We're not doing what we were educated or trained to do. We're on somebody else's turf—and that only makes our anxiety more intense, because so much is riding on the outcome.

We lose our confidence, our enthusiasm, our focus. We freeze up. We brace ourselves mentally for anguish at a minimum, failure as a real possibility.

We're putting ourselves in the dentist's chair, staring at those drills and needles, instead of anticipating that nice, gleaming smile we're going to eventually emerge with.

But wait…. There *is* a better outcome, if we look closer.

Because the problem is simply this: The marketer in us is asleep. Only we can't wake it, because we can't find it. It doesn't look like we think it does; it doesn't reside where we think it is.

We are confused and misdirected because we're looking for what we mistakenly assume the sleeping marketer inside us must be: some whiz-bang, super-creative copywriter, or artsy graphics genius. That person most likely never existed in us, or has long been locked up in the attic of our consciousness, left to wither and die.

After all, we went to law school, or took the financial planner certifying exams, or joined the family real estate business. We chose the path we preferred. So now we think the dormant marketer inside us is some long-lost, invisible, untouchable person who possesses talents that we don't. It's like standing up in a karaoke bar on Thursday night to perform. We all sang in kindergarten, but now some of us cower at the prospect of leaping on stage to belt out a chorus of "Satisfaction." We decided somewhere along the way that we were musically challenged. If we're in that mindset, we *can't* summon up our inner rock star, or inner marketing person—because he or she probably *isn't* in us.

The main purpose of this book is to convince you, the professional in a small practice or firm, that the sleeping marketer in you is someone else entirely. It's someone you *can* feel comfortable with, someone fully competent to handle the job of marketing and growing your business.

The second purpose of this book is to show you how to wake that person up and put him or her to work–attracting new prospects, bringing in new clients, and stimulating more referrals and word-of-mouth.

So here's the deal: the inner marketer in you is… *you.*

You as in the person you are right now, every working day, doing the work that your clients value and respect. You as in the same skill set and mindset you bring to the office each morning along with your Starbucks.

It's the successful professional you already are. Because that same unique quality I referenced earlier—the one that makes you special and valuable to the clients you serve—also makes you of value to the marketplace at large, to that vast, unseen universe of people who will become your next clients.

Every morning you wake up yourself, and that unique quality or skill you possess, and send them out the door to earn yourself a living.

Now you're going to give that person a second job. You're going to ask him or her to do pretty much the same things to *attract* new clients that he or she already do to *serve* the existing ones.

I'll bet no one ever told you before that *that* person could be any good at marketing.

That person as a marketer is asleep. *That* person likely doesn't have flair for creative marketing.

But that person does have an ability to serve the marketplace with a core skill. And so you're going to take that ability and learn how you can use it to market and grow your practice. On your own terms. In a way that makes sense, comes naturally, and is do-able.

So in these pages you're going to wake up him or her. And if you are serious about it, if you follow the system I am about to unfold, you will soon be attracting more prospects, generating more referrals, and bringing in more new business than ever before.

Here's the deal, the very essence of this approach:

1) *Your professional expertise and knowledge is a valuable commodity in the marketplace. Potential clients will pay attention to it and respond to it.*

2) *You can use this situation to your advantage. You can capitalize on it to capture those new clients and grow your business. You can turn it into a business-development tool—into your entire business development/ marketing strategy, even.*

People will pay attention to what you have to say about buying an insurance policy, investing in the stock market, buying or selling real estate, removing warts, or whatever is the topic that you know inside and out. You *are* the expert. (And don't tell me you're under-qualified for this game because you didn't graduate with honors from Harvard, or you don't have your town's most prestigious practice. To 99.99 percent of the world, and to 100 percent of your prospects, you *are* the expert.)

And once they're noticing what you say, they will start paying attention to *you*. Because you'll build your marketing pieces around bits of your advice and wisdom, and start getting them out in front of the market regularly and frequently. When *that* starts happening, you begin to establish a "virtual" relationship with your target market—one that builds and snowballs into more clients, better word-of-mouth, and more referrals.

How to do that—what to say, how to say it, and how to get it out there so the marketplace pays attention, is what unfolds in the following chapters.

And by the way, I'm not going to literally push you "out there." When I speak of getting your expertise in front of people, I'm not going to ask you to have two hundred prospect lunches and three hundred breakfasts a year, or become a published author, or professional speaker. Unless you want to. Nor will I ask you to give away the same service and counsel your clients pay for.

But I *will* show you an easier, smarter way. It's a system whose DNA I've uncovered and explored, through many years of working with clients.

Think of it for now, if you like to wrap a clear, simple label around an important concept, as "Expertise Marketing."

Here's what you need to take away from this chapter:

- You have valuable professional expertise and knowledge.
- Your clients see it, value it, and pay for it.
- Your clients were once prospects—that means there's potentially no difference between a client and a prospect.
- So it follows that prospects will also notice and value your expertise.
- You can use this fact to your advantage to attract new clients and grow.
- The techniques you'll use to do this all play to your strengths—your professional abilities. They will not require you to resort to the discipline of marketing as it is traditionally practiced or to the often-inhibiting expense of it.

3

THE THREE TRAPS THAT CAN DOOM YOUR MARKETING

Ok. You're starting to discover, and wake up, the marketer in you. But just as arising and rolling out of bed in the morning is only half the battle, you have another dragon in your path to slay before you can do some serious business growth work.

Each morning I consider it a victory when I get on my feet, maybe squeeze in a workout, and make it out the door. But no matter how fired up I may feel upon arriving at work, I'm not yet ready to join the daily battle. To be productive, I first have to slay all the dragons within me: The lazy dragon. The distracted dragon. The uncertain, the misdirected, and the unaware dragons. They all have to go before I can move forward.

Similarly, we all have to slay all the erroneous and destructive thoughts, beliefs, and attitudes we've been carrying around as excess baggage for years. Only then can we grow our business effectively and smartly. So let's peer into the dark side of our brains, and explore the negative thoughts and erroneous assumptions you, I, and everyone hold—and the trouble they land us all in. There are five:

1. The false belief that you can't "do marketing" or adequately oversee a marketing employee or vendor, because it's some unfamiliar dark art at which you are clueless.

2. The misguided notion that you must, and will, find a way to muddle through anyhow, and get some slick-looking marketing materials out the door.

3. The dangerous view that marketing has to be self-congratulatory or manipulative of the audience.

4. The incorrect belief that marketing and business development costs a lot because you have to hire expensive people to do it.

5. The wrong assumption that it takes too much time—time you could be working with revenue-producing clients—to market your firm.

Now let's examine the "Three C's"—the big traps you can fall into as a result of these mistaken thoughts.

The "Copycat" Trap

You're busy, stressed, and want to get something done and out the door quickly. So, consciously or unconsciously, you fall back on imitating what others have done. Maybe you even pull out a few brochures that you have saved from competitors, because you like the way they look. Here's the funny part about that one: when I ask professionals how they differ from their main competitors, they can usually rattle off five or six ways pretty quickly. Yet they'll go right to those same competitors' materials and say or think, *Ours should look like this.* But what they're actually thinking, when you analyze it, is a guaranteed set-up for failure. It's as if they're deciding, *We want to show the marketplace that we're different and better… so let's do what everyone else does.* That, of course, makes no sense; if you look like everyone else, the market perceives you as being the same as everyone else. (Did you think those prospects were really going to wait to form a judgment until they reached your finely-crafted paragraph on page nine that explains how you're different?)

Or you think you know what marketing "should" look like, so you try to come up with something that matches your erroneous expectations. What you get is exactly what you unconsciously set out for: a bland, consensus-type piece that looks like everything else—and therefore makes the prospect conclude that yes, you must be about the same as everyone else.

Great. You've convinced the marketplace there is nothing special about you, nothing that makes you stand out. Now you're just another vendor—and when the buying or hiring decision is made, you're at the mercy of which marketing brochure ends up on top of the pile on the client's desk, or which vendor offers the lowest price, or which one went to the same school as the managing partner's spouse.

Sometimes, in doing what you think marketing *should* be, you even wind up broadcasting messages that are harmful to your goal. You may resort to hyperbole and the self-congratulatory, doing the Muhammad Ali act: "I'm the greatest!" Trouble is, that's what so many competitors are saying, too. The marketplace doesn't believe it about them, either, by the way.

Did you ever watch a group of very young boys practice baseball—those of a certain age—old enough to have awareness of the game, but still too young to possess ability to do much with a bat or glove? They step into the batter's box, and immediately begin imitating the mannerisms and moves of the big leaguers they watch on TV. They'll spit on the ground. They'll clutch the bat and wave it around menacingly. They'll even scratch themselves in that way that ballplayers do. They'll do everything but make contact when the pitch is delivered!

That's what it looks like when professional practices and firms fall into the Copycat Trap.

The "Common" Trap

This one includes the things everyone seems to do at one point or another: the tricks-trinkets-tickets gambit. You start with the otherwise sensible idea of putting your name in front of your prospects and clients as often as possible. You order 500 or 1,000 or 10,000 of the latest promotional gimmick. Maybe it's a calendar in December, a highlighter pen in March, a beach ball in June, all imprinted with your name or logo. You send it out. But you've wasted the opportunity, despite all the effort. Why? Three reasons: 1) You've failed to attach anything to your name that might do you some good—such as some example or message that demonstrates how your service benefits the prospect. 2) You've done what everyone does, thus failing to differentiate yourself. 3) You've deployed a tactic that is not associated with a high quality professional service firm. It's what the market expects, and gets, from the local car wash or dry cleaners.

The ballgame/show/concert tickets strategy is fine in its place—a nice way to spend time with, or reward, your best clients or referral sources. But it's a client-retention strategy, not a growth strategy. You can't afford to spend the time or money giving tickets to all the prospects out there whom you want to convert to clients.

The Common Trap often surfaces in the very words you choose to use. A client once put it explicitly to me: "I want our brochure to say who we are, what we do, and why we do it well." Fine, but that's what everyone is saying. Do that, and you've failed to give the marketplace a single reason to pick you ahead of others making the same claim. Think about it: your piece might look and read unique to *you*, but the prospect is probably evaluating three or four competing firms and has all their materials spread out on the table.

If you merely convey that you're good, you're still only one of three brochures sitting on the prospect's desk.

Ask yourself two questions every day:

- "What am I doing today to look and sound different?"

- "What am I doing today to demonstrate how my service benefits my clients?" (Note: this is very different from *telling them*, or trying to persuade them with hyperbole and clever marketing copy. I'll explore that difference in the following chapters; it is crucial to a professional practice's marketing success.)

Why do smart professionals still fall into the Common Trap? I believe it's because of something they have and something they forget. What they have: a burning determination to act decisively and get something out the door that will drum up some business. So they look for a quick fix, and the mail carrier will probably oblige by delivering yet another catalog full of prosaic promotional items. What they forget: to use their imaginations, their common sense, and to take that moment to ask themselves, "How can I be different today?"

The "Crash" Trap

This one befalls almost every firm and practice at some point. You run into a wall. Frustrated, lacking time or sense of urgency, uncertain of how to proceed or what to do, you do… nothing. You stop, frozen. Nothing emanates, nothing happens.

You can construct all kinds of rationalizations, reasons, and excuses for your paralysis. You can ignore it, telling yourself that client service comes first. But nonetheless, there it is. The doubter in you has raised its deceitful, manipulative head and halted you dead in your tracks.

Slaying this particular dragon requires a two-step attitude adjustment. The first step is to discipline yourself—commit to a plan of action, however small the steps may be. The second is to redefine what constitutes action. You have to forget all the stuff that doesn't work—the stuff we've been discussing up to now—and pick up a new game plan. The one that starts with the next chapter of this book.

Now let's take a quick look at some other deadly mistakes, dragons, and wrong paths that I've been alluding to. Any of them can derail business growth.

Once In A While: Doing something once in a while simply doesn't cut it. The marketplace won't even notice you until you've gotten in front of them several times. You don't need me to tell you they're too busy. In your heart, you know they are not sitting around eagerly anticipating the arrival of your next mailer. And even when they do notice you, they may not need you. Just as they may not need to buy a new car this month, they may be perfectly happy at the moment with their current financial advisor, attorney, podiatrist, or insurance broker or with having none. At the moment your annual marketing piece lands on their desk, they've got more bills to pay than savings to invest. They don't know that next month they're going to receive an inheritance, that their podiatrist will announce she's moving to Arizona, or that their car will be totaled. Where does that leave you, if you sent them your annual mailer piece *last* month?

I Don't Have Time: Of course you don't. I don't have time either. No one does. Still…

Here's a partial list of what I *do* have time for in a typical day:

- Eat breakfast at my desk
- Fix my coffee just the way I like it
- Eat a late morning snack at my desk
- Have lunch in the park, if it's a nice day
- Check the newspaper to see how my sports teams did last night
- While I'm at it, read half of the rest of the paper
- Go online to buy tickets to a concert
- Stay online to check on the status of my delayed catalog order
- Check in with my son three times by phone, during his school breaks
- Call my insurance company to inquire why the premium went up
- Schedule an appointment with my doctor
- Cancel this afternoon's appointment with my other doctor—because I'm just too busy today.

Every day I convince myself that I am "too busy" to get around to one or more of the really pressing matters on my to-do list.

Who am I fooling?

I know—and I suspect you know too—that if something is really critical, I can manage to devote fifteen minutes, or half an hour, or an hour to it. Probably every day; certainly two or three times a week.

And that, my friends, is all you need to devote to the marketing system in this book.

I won't attempt to persuade you that marketing and business development is critical to your firm's future. Only you can decide that.

But I can tell you this: if you decide that it is, and you can find just thirty minutes, two or three times a week, you'll have slain the "I don't have time" dragon. And you'll be well down the road to attracting new clients and revenue.

I Can't Afford It: A lot of this one is based on outmoded, or ill-conceived ideas of what marketing used to be. It used to rely heavily on expensive, fancy-pants printed materials, and costly mailings. In the early days of the Internet age, it used to hang solely on creating a gee-whiz web site. Those days are gone. New technologies, new strategies, new ways to use the Internet and media, have created a whole new landscape. That's why the "Awaken The Marketer" program is based entirely on affordable steps that nearly all practices, even the smallest, can manage.

Just Like the Big Guys: Maybe you used to work for the Big Guys. Or you're going after clients who can afford to hire them. Whatever the reason, you're certain you've got to show the market you're as good as those Big Guys. And it starts with having commensurate marketing materials, right? Stop yourself! They'll never believe it, no matter how many times you tell them, until you start to show them. So don't waste time and money trying to look like you're global when you're local. Not only does it backfire, it will run you into the ground financially. You can't outspend the Big Guys. You can't outslick them either in your materials. So why try? You aren't one of them. You pride yourself on telling your prospects you'll service them better than the giants. Stop trying to look like what you're not. A wise communicator, in another context, once put it this way: "They've seen *slick*. They haven't seen *you*." Be you.

Once in my public-relations days, a couple of moneyed ex-Wall Street guys dreamed up a concept for a new franchised fast-food chain. They didn't even have a prototype or a real plan, yet they wanted publicity. And they pulled off some esoteric, murky financial/legal transaction that effectively qualified their corporation to be listed on some stock exchange. They could not fathom why the *Wall Street Journal* would not publish this "news," as it had when the mega-corporations they once worked for did the same maneuver. They couldn't stop looking in the mirror and seeing a twelve-foot giant.

Capabilities and Qualifications: I touched on this one before. You state concisely and accurately what you do, what your credentials are. As if every firm couldn't come up with the exact same thing. So what's your selling point—that all your partners really did graduate college? *Hint: the marketplace assumes you are qualified and competent.*

By the way, beware too the corollary mistake: the "I'm So Great That I Just Have to Tell You I Am" one. If you build your marketing around the message of "We're Great and We Do 'X,'" what do you say next month when you go back to the marketplace? "Hi, We're Still Great, and We Still Do 'X'"? Yet I see many firms do just that. Half their marketing consists of cranking out the next press release or tombstone ad that boasts how "Jenny Jones has joined our firm, so now we're even better." What a waste of time and money! The only people who know Jenny are her parents, friends, and clients—and they already heard about her move. Anyone else who needs to know—send them an e-mail. You'll save effort and expense.

The Best of Both Worlds: A corollary of "Just Like the Big Guys." It goes like this: *We're just like the big firms, except…*

Come on, say it aloud with me. You know it by heart, don't you?

"…except we offer a hands-on personal touch. We have a senior person on every account."

Trust me on this; I've worked with enough service providers to know.

They're all doing this. They're all saying this. So despite best intentions, they've communicated nothing new or meaningful to the prospect.

The "Niche Itch": This one seems to make sense at first. You specialize in something narrow, specific, and in demand. So you'll just tell the world what you do, and why you do it well. Problem: you've defined yourself well, but you haven't made anyone want to buy a relationship of trust with you. Would Madison Avenue promote a new product with an ad that says, "You should buy our new breakfast cereal because it's made with oats, nuts, and honey"? Would the automakers produce a commercial that says, "Our SUV is roomy and less likely to kill you in a crash than a small car"?

Let's Keep Trying 'Til We Get It Right: I know one group that seems to change its logo, its slogan, and its letterhead every time I look. Some businesses are always tinkering with their look, their message, or their tactics, because it never feels quite right. No wonder. They're trying so hard to figure out what the marketplace will respond to, that they miss the one move that always feels right–being true to yourself.

Share Your Bad

What was the worst mistake, or dumbest thing, you ever did in your marketing? Fess up and share it with me in an e-mail. I'll select the best object lessons and, with your permission, publish them on my web site. In return for your honesty (and anonymity if you wish), I'll give you a peek at *my* dumbest mailing. Send to info@Mediaimpact.biz.

So let's recap where things stand.

We're all busily striving to show the marketplace we're better than and different from the competition—and we're just as busily copying each other in our marketing materials and messages, so we come out looking the same.

We're resorting to the fallback default of giving away gimmicks, premiums, and tickets—but if we ever put it to a cost-benefit analysis, we'd probably be dismayed at what we'd see.

Or else we're consumed by doubt, uncertainty, or the belief that we lack time, resources, and ability to do some marketing that's any good. So we're effectively paralyzed, doing nothing or next to nothing. Our marketing plan is to do what we've always done, and then respond to the next proposal opportunity.

And then we wonder: "How come I'm not breaking through the clutter?" "Where are the new clients I thought would be flocking to me?" "Why am I not being heard?"

When you were in school, if you were the math or science whiz or the ace writer, did you ever try to impress people by attempting to act cool, like the star quarterback or the captain of the cheerleaders? Chances are it didn't work any better for you than it did for me. And when did you finally start to fit in, and perhaps even have a cool group of friends? Most likely, it was after you woke up and started being yourself.

It's the same way in business. People pick it up instantly, instinctively, when you're not being you. They see it coming a mile away. And they lock the door, put the fences up. When do they respond to you? When you communicate that you're just being yourself.

I know it often works differently in marketing consumer products like cars, vacations, or computers.

But that's not the line you're in.

For what you do—serving clients, or patients, or customers by giving them the benefits of what you know—you just can't be someone or something else.

So let's get on with the important business of learning how to be yourself in your marketing.

4

BE THE FLAME

Donald Trump was sitting in the audience when my new boss rose to propose a public relations campaign to an eminent group of New Yorkers—the CEOs of Manhattan's most elite and prestigious department stores, plus some of the town's most celebrated real estate barons. It was my third day on the job at a major New York City PR firm, so I was a tag-along as my boss did the heavy lifting.

This crowd's gilded feathers had been sorely ruffled back then by some City Hall policies that were adversely affecting their businesses and, they felt, the quality of life for tourists and New Yorkers. They had hired my new employer to mount a PR campaign to sway the public to their side. This would be no small feat: my new clients were not exactly everyday Joes, and the ultimate target of their ire was a hardy band of hardworking little-guy individuals with whom many New Yorkers were bound to sympathize.

My boss stood up and launched into a carefully developed, richly detailed plan based on all the best tools of the trade. Research would be commissioned, facts assembled, policy papers written, newspaper editors met with—everything in the playbook.

Then Trump stood up from his seat in the crowd. Just minutes earlier, he had clasped my boss on the shoulder and told him, "You guys are doing a great job." Only now he didn't look so pleased.

"We don't need to do any of that!" he said, his trademark flair for the dramatic very much evident.

Heads swiveled and moneyed jaws dropped ever so noticeably. The never-bashful Mr. Trump had interrupted my boss practically in mid-sentence.

"We can get this job done faster," Trump pressed on, impatience apparent in his rising voice. "I'll tell you exactly what we're going to do."

All eyes were riveted in Trump's direction. He wasn't even an officer of the organization, and here he was telling them, and the experts (that would be my boss and me) what to do.

"We're going to hold a press conference next week. And I'm going to stand up there and call the mayor a no-good, blankety-blank, bleepity-bleep for not fixing this problem."

Only he didn't say "blankety-blank."

And he sat down with a flourish, to stunned silence. This crowd wasn't accustomed to such language, or bold talk, in their carpeted Fifth Avenue aeries.

But slowly, one by one, little smiles broke through, and heads started to nod in agreement. These merchant princes had reached the pinnacle of their profession because they shared one trait: an uncanny ability to spot a winner long before it hit the sales floor. Within days, we held our press conference. Trump was the featured star, and he performed as he had promised—minus the salty language. It was the most media-jammed press conference I had ever witnessed, and Trump was the top story that night. Within weeks, City Hall had changed its policies, and before long a new law emerged from the state capital granting my clients further relief.

The deeper moral of this story, to me, is not that being confrontational, flamboyant, and media-savvy pays off in today's world. You know that already.

It's that Trump looked forward eagerly to that moment when he'd stand up before the cameras and blast the mayor. He relished his moment for two reasons. One, he knew it would work. Two, doing things like this is exactly what gets him off.

How did he know it would work? Easy. Whatever you think of Donald Trump as a businessman, person, or celebrity, you won't find a better example anywhere of the power of being yourself. In this case, Trump understood that he could have the media eating out of his hand any time he wanted to. And he knew that by leveraging that power, he could prod City Hall into action.

Now, I am not going to exhort anyone who reads this book to emulate this particular man. Donald Trump, at the time of this incident and for many years after, truly possessed unique value in the marketplace. The rest of us are not Donald Trumps. I've had hundreds of clients over the years, but I only have one story like this one.

But yet…

You can still learn a valuable lesson from this anecdote. Even if you are not as provocative, aggressive, and entertaining, even if you do not share his zest for the limelight or his name recognition, you still have your own unique value in the marketplace.

After all, if you didn't, you wouldn't have a business. Clients wouldn't come back. Like Donald Trump, the marketplace values us most when we are being ourselves.

My friends Ted and Sofia Geier were getting ready for their first appearance on national talk TV. This wasn't exactly starting at the bottom. It was *Oprah*. They hadn't sought her out; she had found them. The Geiers had just started a charitable organization, to honor the memory of their daughter, helping AIDS orphans in Africa. Building on an effort their late daughter had started with her lunch money, they had raised their first $10,000. They knew that Oprah would soon be undertaking a trip to Africa to advance her own causes there. Did I think it would be a good idea, they asked me, to hand their $10,000 over to Oprah for her to deliver in person? And to surprise her by doing it on air?

It was out of the box as a growth strategy for a fledgling non-profit and as a media strategy. You don't go on a show like *Oprah* and surprise the host and producers by deviating from the plan. But the gesture was sincere, genuine—and smart. New to running their own organization and new to the national media spotlight, the Geiers didn't know what the rules were. They were just doing what their hearts were telling them to do. I encouraged them to do it. They did, Oprah loved it, and it was the beginning of a valued ongoing relationship between her and their organization, the Love, Hallie Foundation. It happened because the Geiers trusted in being themselves.

> *To learn more about the Love, Hallie Foundation, visit **www.LoveHallie.org***

And therein lies the key to success in almost anything, reduced to two short words: *Be you.* Funny thing about that: despite all we learn and experience in school, in our careers and lives as adults, it boils down to two words any first grader can read and write readily.

Be you.

Be you, all the time. Not only when you serve your clients and do your work, but when turning your attention to attracting new clients and growing the business.

Bring who you are and what you are to the forefront whenever you are reaching out in any way to prospects, referral sources, or anyone in the marketplace. Remember, *they've seen slick.* Now, show them *you.*

Being you simply means relying on your knowledge, expertise, and values when you go into the marketplace. These three ingredients are the building blocks of your entire approach to business building. This is very different from the normal kind of marketing. Even when done honorably and well, marketing is still based largely on artifice, manipulation, hype, flash, and splash.

Knowledge, expertise, and values. Artifice, manipulation, hype, flash, and splash. They're opposite poles of the spectrum.

If you're in a professional services firm or practice, you need to get to the correct pole—the one that's different from what people normally think of as marketing.

Whenever you enter the marketplace with your expertise as the foundation, you enter it as a resource, not a salesperson. You enter it more comfortably, since you are a professional and not a Madison Avenue mind-manipulator. You enter it ethically and appropriately. You gain and build credibility and trust—the exact two states you must establish to get and keep clients. And because you are more comfortable, you are more likely to remain on task and actually get something constructive done. You have found a direct channel to locate and awaken the marketer in you—the person most qualified and most motivated to go out and get you some new business. And if that's not enough—you enter the marketplace with an infinite supply of raw material. Because when you use your knowledge as the raw ingredient and basis for your whole approach, you will never run dry. You know too much.

Imagine always knowing what to say and do next in your marketing. Imagine not having to approve a new brochure, mailer, or ad every time you want to do something about finding new business.

It reminds me of a memorable line in an otherwise forgettable movie, *Casanova*. Toward the end of this convoluted celluloid tale of Casanova's exploits and adventures, a young acolyte begs him to reveal the secret of his success. How, he asks, does Casanova get all those women flocking to him?

"Be the flame, not the moth," Casanova replies.

After years of working with clients who wanted to grow their organizations, I began to understand what they were doing right and what wasn't working for them. Looking closely at all their collective experiences, triumphs, and frustrations, I saw patterns emerge. I realized I had uncovered the DNA of a system to market and grow a professional services firm. I don't think I've discovered anything breathtakingly groundbreaking. I certainly haven't invented anything. All I've done is observe, reflect, and distill my learnings into succinct form.

It boils down to three steps I believe will make it easier, more comfortable, more impactful, and more successful for many smaller professional practices—and maybe you—to market and attract clients:

1) *You'll draw on the same pool of professional knowledge and expertise you already possess and use every day. You'll serve it up to the marketplace of prospects and potential new clients in small, timely, manageable slices that will pique interest and attract attention.* Slices that will be easy (not to mention inexpensive) for you to create and deliver—and easy for recipients to receive, open, and look at. These bits of your knowledge—and not the slick promo-speak marketing stuff that works for bigger businesses—will become the center of your entire marketing effort. So you'll devote 90 percent of your marketing energy, budget, and output to this type of material. This—all that you know—is what the marketplace wants, craves, and remembers. Why? Because they've got problems or needs they want solved. Because when they find the person (you) who can help them do that, they will value you greatly. Call it "Expertise Marketing" if you will, as I suggested earlier. You can still cover the inevitable self-promotion we all sometimes find irresistible in the remaining 10 percent.

2) *Regularly, you'll create simple but effective messages, materials, strategies, tactics, and tools that are based on your subject matter expertise. You will send these out frequently, in a variety of familiar forms, such as e-mail notes, letters, and short, focused articles.* In this way you'll constantly stay top-of-mind with prospects, referral sources, and with the marketplace in general. Which is where you need to be since it can take months for a prospect to reach the "buy" decision.

3) *By repeating these steps, you will build virtual relationships with prospects, referrers, and the marketplace.*

Many of these relationships will blossom into client engagements as you nurture and develop them. Not only will you be communicating often—but you'll be talking *to* them, not *at* them, so they're more likely to listen. You'll now be connecting your own professional uniqueness and core strengths to what the marketplace cares about and needs. Of course, you'll develop these new prospect relationships wisely, to build the awareness and trust that turns strangers into clients. It's the same as meeting two or three times, or talking on the phone with prospects, as you gradually win them over and close the deal. Only it's on a much wider scale, because you'll be reaching far more people with your materials than you could ever connect with in a month of sit-downs and prospecting calls.

That's really the whole system. I'm going to devote the rest of this book to showing you how to build these relationships. So now you know what's coming—and what you can expect. It's time to meet...

THE *mPOWER* SYSTEM

Share Your Best

Is there one marketing tactic, or piece, or strategy that really worked for you? That made the phone ring? Or, is there one piece you received yourself that was so good you still remember it? Share it with me and our readers (anonymously if you wish). Just send it to info@Mediaimpact.biz, and I'll post or publish the best of them.

5

A SMARTER, BETTER WAY: USING THE mPOWER SYSTEM

The mPOWER system is based on the four M's. They are:

1. Mindset
2. Marketplace
3. Message
4. Multiply

Mindset: Refers to how you think about marketing and business development. In a word: differently. In a way that is professional, appropriate, and non-manipulative or gimmickry-based. If that makes sense to you—if you can envision marketing your firm, practice, or organization in this way—you are well on the road to adopting the mPOWER mindset.

If you wake up tomorrow, and the day after, and next week, still envisioning it, you're there. You have internalized the mPOWER mindset. You are able to embrace these concepts and integrate them into your daily thinking and actions. You are able to begin serious growth.

Mindset also means that you are *always* thinking about marketing and business development. I once asked the CEO of a major, nationally-known nonprofit advocacy group how much of his time he devoted to marketing, media, and public relations. "Fifty to 70 percent," he told me without hesitation. Think about that a minute. On his plate at any given moment: dealing with fundraising, relations with his board, overseeing research and taking a stand on national issues, testifying at government hearings, and running a large organization. He fits all of that into less than half his day. It's no surprise that his organization is *always* quoted in the media when his organization's topic of concern is in the news. He's always making sure of it.

I don't suggest you shrink your client service time to a minority of the available hours, but this example does dramatize how seriously the pros take media and marketing. The mindset: You're always doing or planning the next marketing/business development move. While you're *waiting* for something great to happen, you're *making* something small happen. Every day.

Mindset: You stop talking down to your audience. You forget the hard sell. You stop thinking that the goal is to manipulate, cajole, con, or wear them down to become your next client. You treat them with dignity and respect. You move from hyperbole to humility, from image to *identity*. You are comfortable with who you are and what you must do to market intelligently. The mPOWER mindset takes hold when you can look at yourself in the mirror each morning and tell yourself—without experiencing any pain or disappointment—that the marketplace doesn't care about you. It cares about its own needs. Which is fine. Now you can smile and say, "That's great, because I'm the one who can meet those needs."

The mindset: "From this day forward, I am a resource for the marketplace. As I share with them, they will come to respect me, value me, hire me, and refer me."

Marketplace: The second M builds on your awareness that in marketing it's all about *them*, not *you*. So you're going to be thinking about them every day. Not about how you are going to sell yourself and try to impose your marketing messages on them, but actually about *them:* Who they are, what they need, and how you can best provide it. Sometimes I think we all envision our prospects or target market as prey to hunt or trap. We want to snare them, bag them. No more. The mPOWER system says that instead we want to enlighten them, help them. In that way, they'll truly become ours.

You'll need to know who they are, how they think, and how to relate to them smartly. You'll need to know how to build relationships with them, before you meet them face to face or even interact with them on the phone or by e-mail.

You also need to know this: most prospects want three things from you.

They want your *expertise*. That's no surprise, I hope.

Second, unfortunately, during the time they are still prospects, they want you to *go away*. Let's not be shocked or offended. You and I want all those marketing messages in *our* face from morning or night to go away, too, don't we?

Now the good news: these two aren't as incompatible as it first seems. They don't really want you to disappear. They just want you to hover somewhere in the background until they need you, kind of like parents watchfully guiding a toddler's earliest steps. Prospects usually don't want to know the warning signs of skin cancer until there's a mole on their cheek. They don't want to hear about rolling over their 401(k) until they change jobs. They don't want to learn the ins and outs of inheritance taxes until Grandma dies.

But when any of these events occur, you sure do want to be the one whose name they remember, don't you? Hence the third thing your market wants from you: they just want you to be *patient*, and be there for them when they're ready. Just as the toddler wants Mom and Dad as soon as the going gets rough.

Now let's look at who this marketplace actually consists of.

The people in your universe fall into different categories. I like to think of this universe as a pyramid. At the bottom, the *You-never-knows:* everyone you know and want to stay in touch with—though you couldn't ever rationally explain why in business terms.

For an expanded, printable version of the pyramid in this section that recaps the key information, click on **www.MediaImpact.biz/resources/pyramid**

They will probably never be clients, they have never referred a client or even a prospect, but you think, "You never know," and so they sit for years in your database. That's OK—hey, you never know—as long as you don't devote too much energy or expense to the effort. Go ahead and send them a holiday card and another mailing once a year, if it makes you feel better. These people are basically your contacts, nothing more.

Next up the ladder: *leads.* They are the people you met at last month's networking breakfast who expressed at least some minimal interest in what you do and offer. Vague, undefined, modest interest with no specific next step on the horizon is the defining characteristic of this set. You'll want to put them in your database, sending them all that you normally send the rest of your target market. But there's no benefit to going further—to customizing your messages or reaching out personally to them. The payoff usually does not justify it. Generally speaking, there are too many of them, with too few likely to ever deliver a meaningful payoff, to make it worthwhile to go to extra lengths. But by including them on your mailing list, you'll maintain contact with them several times a year, increasing the likelihood that they will move up to the higher elevations, where…

The *prospect* resides. Leads do not become prospects until they express serious, specific interest in what you do and in the possibility of working with you, and you have had a preliminary discussion about this. In the consumer world, someone who wants to buy a new dress walks into a store and buys one. But in the professional services arena, someone typically either becomes a client very quickly—they have a specific, probably urgent need right now—or they can remain a prospect for weeks or months before becoming a client. Prospects are critical to your growth. It is essential to identify them when they come along, reserve a special spot for them in your mind, heart, and database, and give them special treatment. You'll be connecting with them regularly, as you'll see in this and the next chapter. It's just important to remember that you can't make them be ready for you; only they can. Your job is to remain on their minds, sending reminders that are informative as opposed to intrusive, until they are ready.

Approaching the stratosphere, we reach the *client*. Some of your clients may be active—they are working with you regularly—while others may be inactive: months or even years can go by before you hear from them, but when they need you, they call. Talk about a group that deserves special care and attention! Not only are they the lifeblood of your business, but they are more likely than strangers to engage you for your expanded or additional services as you add them to your repertoire. They are also excellent potential referral sources. So let's give them something extra. Whatever you start sending your leads and prospects (and you'll have a good idea of what that is after the next chapter), you'll go one better with clients. They expect to receive more: they are already paying for your services. Perhaps it is more detailed or specific information than you'd share with non-clients, or guidance and knowledge that specifically fits their industry, profession, or market.

At the apex of our pyramid sits the referral source. Let's come up with a better name for them—one that acknowledges the powerful lift they can give to your practice. A good, reliable, enthusiastic referral source is a *sustainer* for your firm. A productive one can practically keep your business going by steadily feeding you new clients. Sustainers, if they're not clients, are most often in professions that work in fields related to yours: the banker who refers the lawyer, the real estate agent who recommends the mortgage broker. Step one with these important people—and it sounds elementary, but many of us forget to do it: Know who your sustainers are. Analyze your client roster to see who's sending you business, and how much. Make sure they're in your database—in a special category all to themselves. You're obviously going to give this group extra attention too—but a special kind of attention. Sustainers have their own interests and needs related to their own profession and business. You can't send them the same things you send to your own target market. Example: if I am an attorney and my *client target* is home buyers, I might be sending my database a series of e-mails with basic tips on how to deal with the main legal issues when buying a home. But if my *sustainers* are real estate agents, those messages would fall flat and miss the mark; this audience is far more knowledgeable than my home buyers. The agents have totally different perspectives and needs. So I'll send them a set of messages, perhaps something to update them on recent court cases and new laws that may affect their brokerage business. Anything that's information they *need*.

Will the sustainer who receives this message call tomorrow and hire me to handle just the matter I mentioned in my message? Occasionally, but more often not. And that is fine—because my long-term objective is simply to stay top-of-mind with these sustainers. I want them to remember me next week when someone asks if they know a good real estate lawyer.

To be *hired*, you need to be *remembered*. To be remembered, you need to *remind* your audience that you're out there. You also need to be *noticed* each time you do it. To be noticed, since you can't afford to hammer your way in intrusively and repeatedly like Madison Avenue with constant repetition, you need to be a *welcome* arrival in their inbox, mailbox, or voicemail. To be welcome, you need to be *useful* to them. Let's boil it down to a simple formula:

That's what I mean by marketplace focus.

Useful
Welcome
Noticed
Reminded
Remembered

+

HIRED

To follow this formula, you need to be thinking about your marketplace all the time: what concerns, issues, wants, and needs are on their minds this month, this week, today? What's new in their world that wasn't even on their radar screens last summer? And, what new information have *I* acquired, what new developments am I up on of because of my professional awareness, that my target market needs to know? This is where the third, and perhaps most crucial, M comes in:

Message: Sure, it's easier to just send out a standard self-promotional message, like everyone else does. But where do *you* file those messages—if they even reach you—when *you* receive them?

Having a different message from the competition is what sets you apart, gets you noticed and remembered. Here's a useful way to grasp the difference between the traditional—and commonplace—marketing message, and what you'll be doing. The *old school* message counts on your repeatedly telling the marketplace what you do (as if that's enough reason to hire you) and how you're so darned good at it (as if you, not they, know best on whom they should spend their money). A better approach: show the marketplace you are *useful*.

Old School Message: "What We Do"

New School Message: "How What We Do Benefits You "

The act that sets you apart, when you follow the mPOWER system, is that you put your message into practice—living it on a daily basis. You don't *tell* the marketplace who you are and why they need you; you *show* them. A young Bob Dylan did this well in one of his early songs:

"I'm a poet…

And I know it"

He told us by showing us.

So you're going to show your prospects that you can benefit them by sending them marketing materials that demonstrate it.

Every time you send something out, ask yourself this question:

"Is this stuff useful to someone?"

And what *is* useful? That's easy: What you *know* is useful, not how great you want everyone to think you are (though, of course, you are).

Depending on your profession, you know: How to save on taxes... How to select the right insurance product... How to spare knees from excessive wear and tear... How to identify a good buy in the real estate market... Whether or not it's smart to step into the global stock markets this year... How to protect your assets when starting a small business.

One more twist to this message stuff: We all know *too* much—about our professional subject matter expertise, at least. We can talk shop for hours with our peers and have a great time. But you know when you've gone too deeply with a client, a prospect, or even a stranger—the glazed look surfaces on their faces and you know you're losing them. At a cocktail party, you get immediate market feedback: the person you're talking to starts glancing about for someone else to engage. So think of the different levels of detail you speak from as you talk to strangers, clients, and other professionals in your field. In expertise marketing, you're aiming for the "stranger" level—the most essential, timely, and practical snips of your knowledge. In marketing, you don't have the benefit of seeing the glazed look/averted gaze feedback from the other person. So you have to figure out in advance how much depth to give them.

Usually, it's way less than you think. The average prospect or sustainer, at this point in your relationship, doesn't need even 2 percent of what you know. So you're going to dish out just the basic, most crucial information in the shortest form possible. That's smart marketing in two ways: You're going to make it easy for your audience to get what you're saying, and it's way easier for you to actually get some marketing out the door. You're not going to be writing four-thousand-word scholarly articles, I promise! Writing less is easier once you learn how to do it. In the next chapter, I'll show you how to make this part *really* easy.

WHY PROSPECTS CALL

Estes Park, Colorado, is a resort town teeming with realtors. Robby Carson of Estes Park Realty stands out from the pack by using his advertising and promotion to give consumers free, useful information.

"How To Choose a Real Estate Agent" is the headline for a typical ad he'll run. Instead of the ordinary broker's ad with pictures of appealing houses, his ad consists of nothing but text with practical advice—and a phone number to call to learn more in a free report he'll send to anyone who requests it.

Enough people call to build the business nicely. The firm receives about twelve leads a week just from this one strategy. People who might never call a broker, because they're not quite ready to buy, are eager to pick up the phone for a free information report.

"There's no commitment. They call out of curiosity," Robby says.

When they do, he reaches out to learn more about their real estate needs and plans. Relationships develop.

"There's no smoke and mirrors, no tricks," he says. "It's a way to provide consumers with things they need."

"This," he adds, "is Sales 101: What Can We Do Different?"

Alright, let's examine where we are. You've now determined what you know, and you've identified people in the marketplace—*potential new clients and sustainers!*—who want to learn it. You've started to figure out how to simplify, condense, and package what you know, so those people might actually welcome hearing from you.

You're already in a better place than all your competitors who are no doubt busy this very moment, trying to concoct yet another flashy, clever, and probably costly way to barrel the next promotional piece the market *doesn't* want past all the barriers to getting noticed. *Happy hunting, competitors! While they're at it, you're heading in another direction. You're going to do some expertise marketing.* Now, you just have to learn how to get that expertise noticed. That brings us to the final M.

Multiply: How many times have you heard this (or said it yourself)?

- We tried a marketing campaign, but it didn't work.
- I made up a nice brochure and mailed it out, but nothing happened.
- We tried PR—it didn't get us anything.

All too often, it's just as they (or you) said it: you *did* try it—once.

Forgive me if I'm breaking bad news to you, but here it is: In the game of marketing and business development, hardly anything works if you do it only once.

You already know this. Guys especially know how easily the marketplace can ignore or reject someone. They've been experiencing it since the first time they asked out the cheerleader in high school and got the cold shoulder.

Guys: Did any of us stop trying to date or give up on romance, because the first girl we asked out said no?

So why are so many of us trying out a marketing tack once—and then abandoning it?

You also know that once doesn't work because you know how many times you've seen the same commercial, or the same ad, or gotten the same annoying solicitation mailer. You know that the big players, the organizations with the swollen budgets, are going to come at you again and again. They understand, as we all do, that they need to get their message in front of you seven times before you even notice it—much less act on it. They understand this so well that they spend millions of dollars every week on advertising something you literally could not buy if your life depended on it. I'm referring to the TV and print advertising for blockbuster new movies that starts three to six weeks before opening day. You already knew the movie was coming, you now know when it opens, and you probably decided whether or not you want to see it. But there it is, night after night, on your screen anyway.

No small organization can afford to even play this game, much less compete effectively in it. You can't buy your way to name recognition with advertising. And let's stop dreaming that prospects are going to save that slick brochure we sent them last winter, or rip out that ad we placed a year ago, until they are ready to hire your services.

But you can achieve repetition—and don't kid yourself, achieving it is essential to success—in your own way. The small-size professional practice way. Which means the low-budget, high-value-to-audience way. You can create a system to get yourself out there often enough, to be in front of their eyeballs when they are finally ready. Ready to upgrade to a larger home, or get the kids' teeth fixed, or buy that life insurance policy, or whatever fills their needs.

You're going to do this by building those "virtual relationships" I talked about in chapter 2. And you'll do it at a low cost.

Hence this final M, *multiply.* All it means is that you're going to do your best to get something basic and simple out into the marketplace as often as you can—once a month ideally. It also means you're not going to send it out in the same envelope—or in the same form at all—every time. You're going to multiply your delivery materials and tactics, too.

I know this notion may frighten you half silly. If so, which of the following are you thinking: *Write something every month?... I can't do that/I can't afford that/I don't have time/No one is interested/I have no one to send it to/It's too complicated/I don't have enough material to work from.*

So, here's my plan: *twenty minutes and zero dollars a month, or whatever small amount your budget permits... a target list of nobody but people who already know you and like you... simple messages that are natural and easy for you to create... information that* everyone *in your market wants to know.*

It turns out that this marketing stuff only feels hard when you start with old-school thinking, when you go back to believing that marketing is something only the professionals can do, with those black-magic secrets they learned in MBA school.

Not true! You can multiply too, and on the terms I just set out for you.

Step by step, you'll see how in the next two chapters.

Recap Time

I've covered a lot of ground in this chapter. What matters most: When you come at this whole marketing thing from a mindset of expertise-sharing, you're on familiar turf. No longer are you captive of your weaknesses, fears and dislikes, or gaps in your skills. No longer are you captive of the process of working with an agency, which may or may not fully grasp what makes you unique and what resonates with your marketplace. That's good for a second reason: working with an agency still inherently requires you to review and approve stuff like designs, slogans, materials, and brochures—the stuff you just aren't attuned or trained to evaluate smartly.

When you awaken the marketer hidden in you instead, and leverage the mPOWER approach, you're like a sports team with the home field advantage. You know the territory, and you can recognize and handle the particular individual quirks of the playing field, because it's yours. You're waking up and having breakfast under your own roof. You're just better prepared and more comfortable. So while you still might not win every game, you're going to do better than you ever dreamed possible.

6

WHAT IF YOUR PROSPECTS ACTUALLY LISTENED TO YOU?

Just how *do* you do all that I've just talked about? How do you make something happen in your business development, yet still devote the bulk of your time to revenue-producing service, as you must?

Welcome to the here's-what-to-do chapter.

I'll aim to keep it as simple and straightforward as possible for now. Feel free to embellish and enhance on the basics as you become proficient.

Fortunately, there's a convenient way of making sure it stays simple. That's because all marketing and business development eventually distills down to three words:

WHO

WHAT

and HOW.

That's WHO you need to reach, and WHAT you need to send them. I'll explore these in this chapter. In the next chapter I'll cover HOW you get it to them.

Who:

I talked extensively in the previous chapter about your market-place, the people you need to connect with. It's time to start. Pull out your database and gaze into it. Do you even *have* a database? In electronic form, using simple software that you're comfortable using? I'm fine these days with Outlook's Contacts component. I've used ACT! happily also. Plug your names into whichever one you use. Your prospects, your leads, your sustainers—pile them all in, if they're not yet there. Remembering all we've discussed about having a menu of message delivery methods, include it all: mailing addresses, phone, fax, e-mail. Missing the data? This might be a good task for an admin or a temp to tackle. Or, remember *marketing mindset,* and turn the opportunity into a real connection. Personally craft a fax to everyone whose e-mail address you lack, or make a quick phone call: "Hi, I'm David, the real estate guy you worked with when you bought your home. Just updating my records. If you send me your e-mail address, we can keep in touch down the road, and I'll send you an article on ten easy tips for increasing the value of your house."

Make sure your database provides a basic capability for sorting your names by broad categories. But don't make this part too complicated; don't let it slow you down. Now that you know the difference between a lead, a prospect, and a sustainer, you might want to create separate categories for each within your database, so you can send them separate mailings—or send on a different schedule. Later on, you may want to sort your entries by their particular characteristics or the kinds of service you provide them. Allison Accountant might set up distinct database categories for the primary industries or professions she serves, such as attorneys, insurance people, and construction contractors. Then, as she grows more proficient and comfortable with database expertise marketing, she can target each group with a message tailored just for them: "Five Steps Building Contractors Should Take Now That Congress Has Enacted A Brick Tax." Patrick Planner might create one group of clients and prospects who tend to need active day-to-day investment counsel, another group for those who are more long-term focused on investing for retirement.

But to repeat, don't fuss too much about this now. It'll just become another task that gets in the way of achieving your goals.

By the way, are you one of the many who finally muster the courage to toss all those useless names from your list (bye to that chatty carburetor salesman from Oklahoma City) and trim down to the true prospects actually worth your attention—only to see with dismay your list shrink to itty-bitty size?

Please, hurt not, fear not. Do not feel discouraged. Even if you find yourself staring at a skimpy roster of ten or twenty names, a third of whom are your relatives and college roommates. First of all, as you follow the tactics and techniques I'll cover in the next chapters, your list will grow handsomely and happily. Second, even with just a small number of names for now, you're going to be communicating with them in a whole new way. They are going to notice, listen, and think about you as they never have before. And almost from the get-go, some of them will be passing your name on to others they know.

Besides, in the unlikely event you do find yourself with just ten or twenty true prospects, think of it this way: you can either have twenty names and do nothing about it, or you can have twenty names and do something to help yourself. Which path will you choose?

What:

Now, exactly what *do* you send your marketplace to showcase your expertise, be useful, yet stop short of the level of guidance and detail best reserved for your work sessions with paying clients?

You do this:

STEP 1: *Identify your Subject Matter Expertise*, or SME for short. You have vast amounts of professional knowledge—too much for the marketing task at hand. In your mind, identify the four best, timeliest, most-relevant-to-clients *specific* topics you know well. If you're a financial planner or investment professional, you've passed a series of credentialing exams. If you're a lawyer you've passed the bar; an accountant the C.P.A. exam. And you've kept up with the field. Ask yourself this question: "Of all that knowledge, what's most useful in my business right now?" If you're an investment adviser working with high-income breadwinning parents, it might be maximizing tax-deferral opportunities, or saving for children's college expenses, or strategies for retirement investing. It's probably not the esoteric details of recent tax court decisions. Think it through and pick your handful of best topics. This, for marketing purposes, will be your SME—the basis of all you do from here on to attract new clients and stimulate more referrals. Make sure your choices relate to the needs and concerns of both your prospects and your sustainers as well as clients.

What are clients talking and caring most about these days? What's in the newspapers, on TV news, about your topic? What's brewing in the halls of government or the courts that your clients need to know about? What was the next new thing that everyone was talking about at your professional association's annual conference in San Diego last summer? That's what you want to share and use.

STEP 2: *Break down your SME into the best small, manageable slices you can.* This is critical. Even after condensing your vast knowledge into four SME topics for marketing, you still know far too much for your own good—when it comes to marketing, that is. Just as you wouldn't try to confuse clients with interesting but unnecessary side issues when you work with them, you can't overload non-clients with information in your expertise marketing.

Is this a new concept to you? I don't think so. I believe you already shift your level of detail back and forth unconsciously all week long, as you go about advising clients, meeting prospects, and chatting on the plane with the passenger at your side. But if you're having trouble envisioning how to apply it to marketing, here's an example: If you were an accountant and someone hired you to come in the week after Thanksgiving, and spend two or three hours examining their affairs and advising them on year-end tax moves and strategies, you could do it practically in your sleep. If they had the interest and the money, you could probably go on for another hour or two once you warmed up to the topic, couldn't you? Well, suppose you only had time to send them an e-mail with some bullet points? It might look like this:

- Defer any discretionary income
- Maximize contributions to your 401(k)
- Check to see if you could get bitten by the Alternative Minimum Tax
- Make a gift to your children now rather than later

HE DIDN'T HAVE TO CALL THE MEDIA

 Bill Bengen is a certified financial planner from El Cajon, California. Years ago he searched in vain for reliable information to share with his clients on preparing for retirement. He found little—so he started doing his own research.

What he did was good enough to get published in professional journals, then a book. Soon Bill was making a name for himself nationally as an expert. The media started calling him. Whenever they did, he gave them as much time and attention as they needed—often going the extra mile to create spreadsheets just for their stories. As a result, he got even more media interviews and publicity. "I never sought them out—they found me," he says.

Bill told the *Wall Street Journal* he was "astounded" by the visibility he received—for free. (For the article about him they did, he invested about four hours of time assisting the reporter. He was featured prominently.)

Fueled by the exposure and the top search rankings in Google that followed, his phone rang increasingly—and Bill says he now no longer seeks out new clients.

"It helped me build my practice," he explains. "I was listed with pages of reference, and it developed an aura of professionalism for me."

Or if you're a real estate broker, you might want to say a few words on "Four easy ways to increase the value of your home before putting it on the market." Could you talk about that for an hour? Probably. Could you also shrink it down to five minutes worth of tips to a client while you're driving them to see a property? I think so.

Or maybe you sell air conditioners. Could you riff for a quick moment on "Three signs that you need a new air conditioner?"

And that's how I'm proposing you market, as well. You might send your prospects an e-mail with just those suggestions above, and a link to your web site for more detailed information on each topic—or an offer to call you for more advice. Or, you might send a series of five e-mails, once a week, with a paragraph—no more—on each point.

This task of breaking down your knowledge into little mini-bits is absolutely essential. Without it, you will fail in one of three ways:

- You will do nothing, because the task of writing a full page is too daunting (but anyone can knock out one little paragraph—and if you really think you can't do this, dictate your thoughts to a colleague or employee and have them write it up for you to edit).
- You will do it badly, because you are trying to write too much and you are not a professional writer.
- You will lose the audience with too much detail—the equivalent of cocktail party eyes glazing over.

When you summarize-condense-distill and shrink down your SME, you make your advice look breathtakingly simple and easy—both to receive as a target and for you to create. Too many of us struggle to achieve this effect. Getting your arms around the concept is so tough for most of us. It's because we know so much… we are trained and conditioned to know more, say more, think more.

Please—for marketing and business development purposes only—go against your instincts and give it a try. Examples of this basic, no-frills, no-complications approach to communication surround us everywhere. Think *USA Today* factoids and graphic charts. Think magazine cover headlines ("Ten Ways to Lose Ten Pounds!"). Think headline crawls on the bottom of your screen on ESPN or cable news. The folks at CNN and Fox know a whole lot more about the story than they're sharing at the moment, but they realize that all *you* want to know just now are the few words currently scrolling across the bottom of your picture screen. You'll get the rest of it at another time.

Please. Understand that the professionals in the media make their money by following this crucial keep-it-simple approach. Think like you're a magazine cover headline writer, or a cable news producer, when you do your marketing. Then you can act like an in-depth commentator when you're with clients.

When I was a kid, my parents took me to Hershey, Pennsylvania, where they make the chocolate. I was agog. Inside the factory were the hugest vats imaginable. I had never seen so much chocolate in one place; I was awed by the industrial and logistical prowess it took to create this massive confection-producing operation. Yet for all its skill at producing candy in massive quantities, look at what comes out at the end of Hershey's assembly line—little tiny bars and kisses you can grasp in your hand.

Hershey knows it has to break down its product into tiny bits to get it into the marketplace's hands. You as a professional have to do the same with your product—your knowledge—when you're marketing.

By the way, short and sweet does not mean shallow and superficial. You can say it in a few words, or sentences, or paragraphs and still be insightful, on point, and helpful. It takes a little practice. I know. When I started in newspapers, I wrote for a paper that liked to run long stories. Then I switched to one that favored short news items. How do you explain a complicated crime, a sophisticated political issue, in just three hundred or four hundred words? At first I struggled. But I saw that it could be done, and I practiced until I could do it with the best of them.

Next time you see a brief item in the news about some major new medical study, notice how the newspaper got it down to about three or four inches of what you really need to know. And they probably did it in two or three hours, tops. The study's authors, in contrast, invested years of their lives and probably produced enough words and data to fill a small phone directory. They were working and writing for the medical community. Same information, different levels of detail and accessibility for different audiences and purposes.

I'm not expecting you to acquire the same proficiency in this art as a professional journalist. But I do know, from having worked with many clients who'd be the first to admit they aren't great writers and don't need to be, that most any businessperson or professional can master this.

How do you get accustomed to this challenge of condensing your knowledge down to its essence? Easy. Just listen to yourself.

What do you say to non-clients you meet at a cocktail party, to your seatmate on the late-night flight back home to Jacksonville? In these settings and countless others, you're unconsciously performing the same act of editing down your knowledge. Only you're doing it in verbal form.

Somebody in New York overheard this exchange on the supermarket deli counter line. Shopper to meat slicer: "Slice it thin enough so I can watch TV through it."

To us outsiders, that sounds silly. But that can be how thin the marketplace wants your stuff.

Yes, I am asking you here to spend five or ten minutes thinking about this stuff. This—right here—is the hard part.

But doesn't it sound easier than devoting hours to overseeing the creation and production of that slick new marketing brochure that you probably can't afford anyway? Or that ad campaign that's unlikely to pay for itself?

Here's how this might play out for a commercial real estate broker with a great track record and expertise in one specific niche. Let's consider what Brian Broker, who wants to reach owners of the kind of properties he specializes in, will do. Having talked to many such owners, he knows that the vacancy rate is all this crowd seems to be talking about these days. So, moving from the broad picture to the small slice and identifying the market's current hot button, he thinks through his game plan like this:

My field ⇨ Commercial Real Estate

   My niche ⇨ Retail Strip Mall Leasing

      My market ⇨ Owners

         My market's concern ⇨ Vacancy Rates

            My next marketing piece ⇨ *two, one-line observations about the current state of vacancy rates this season in my town's retail strip malls, and two tips on what owners should do now.*

Having identified your best topics, how do you add the most value? You can convey information—that's always useful. You can apply your knowledge and make some sense of that information for your in-the-dark clients—even better. Or, best yet, you can apply *wisdom* and offer some clear, compelling interpretation and guidance. Here's the model:

Type of Message	Perspective	Value
Information	Ground Level View	Acceptable
Knowledge	10,000 feet	Expected
Wisdom	30,000 feet	Unstoppable!

It's golden when your area of expertise and your client base's backgrounds align. I had a client in accounting who scored home runs consistently by getting his articles on trends in the real estate industry—his client base, which he understood thoroughly—published by a leading newspaper. Another client, a law firm, delivered presentations and wrote articles for the insurance industry—their market. The knowledge and wisdom they shared was so narrow and specific that there couldn't have been more than a thousand companies in the world interested in it.

But for those thousand targets, what this law firm served up was invaluable.

One caveat: you can't fake this stuff. Don't decide that you're going to start talking about junk bonds if you're in the business of selling insurance annuities. One, you lack credibility from the start—and the market knows it. Two, your lack of stature to comment on the issues at hand will show through, no matter how hard you try to mask it. I once worked with a brilliant attorney who was nationally renowned in his particular area of tort litigation—he had even handled several famous, high-media visibility cases. Then he decided he'd wade into writing about politics and national policy. I can still hear the echo of his gasps of disappointment when no one paid attention.

It reminds me of the day I was waiting in a parking lot with my son Jack, then five, for a ride home. In one of the shrub planters, sadly, lay a dead bird. Wishing to shield Jack from such unpleasantness, I told him, "That bird is asleep," and I steered him over to the next bench. When our ride arrived, Jack detoured back to the planter, leaned into it, and said in a voice aimed squarely at me, "Bye-bye, dead bird."

You can't fool the marketplace. Even when it's still in kindergarten.

One final twist: remember when I talked about sustainers and their importance to you? Treat your key referral sources accordingly in developing your messages. All that means is that you'll create tips, advice, and wisdom that relate specifically to them. Another client I had, an accountant, did most of his work for small businesses. But he got nearly all his clients from law firm referrals. So we developed a little system for him to regularly send lawyers brief e-mail reminders and mailers with useful information specifically relevant to accounting issues that law firms might face. (Fortunately, he knew his stuff well enough to hold forth intelligently on the topic.) *Not once did he ask them to do anything for him, or attempt to sell his firm's services to them.* It was just, "Here's something you might want to know." Period. End of communication.

The more he did it, the more the referrals flowed in.

7

LET'S FINALLY *DO* SOMETHING

You finally can see the goal line in sight when you reach the last stage of the formula I laid out in the previous chapter, the part that covers…

How:

It's now time to step up and start doing some marketing. Getting something done has to feel truly do-able, or you'll let it slide by. Now is the moment I need to reassure you that it *is* do-able. Here's why it is:

- You're going to use simple, everyday kinds of communications, like regular e-mails, postcards, and letters.
- All you need to say in them is very simple, elementary bits of information, insight, or advice—things you are entirely comfortable writing and saying.
- You're going to send these simple pieces as often as makes sense, to those people you've decided are important to you. You won't kill yourself trying to do more.

Let's start with a goal. *Your goal is to take one action a month to attract new clients and stimulate more referrals.*

That action will be to send your target list something brief, simple, and easy to create.

OK, to do something once a month, you'll need twelve topics for one year. Don't be intimidated. You don't need to find them all at once, unless you prefer to. It works just as well to pick a topic on the spot each month, or—as I do often—to jot down a thought whenever it occurs to you (as will start happening, once you get into this routine). Coming up with topics should *never* become a time-consuming task. It's just not worth it. Once again, you'll have to trust me on this: you know so much about your area of expertise, that pretty much *anything* you select to share a few sentences on will be valuable to your audience. Personally, I'll just trust on faith that something will come along for me. And it always does. When the time comes to pick my topic for the month, I turn my Internet radio or iPod on. One song's worth of time is all I give myself to select a topic. Song ends, I'm done deciding.

"OK, Ned," I can hear you thinking, "You find it easier than I do to come up with topics, with you being a writer, and all."

Fair enough. But I can show you the shortcuts and tricks I use and that anyone can deploy. Here's how to come up with twelve topics a year, whether your thing is trusts and estate law, retirement investments, refinishing antique furniture, selling insurance annuities, or business-to-business translation services:

Allow yourself to fantasize for a moment that you're the editor of some really trendy magazine. Only it's not about celebrities, sports, or movies. It's about your actual professional topic, your SMEs. As editor, besides going to lots of fancy parties and publishers' lunches, you'll need to show up at the office and do a little work now and then. You'll need to come up with some very specific, intriguing ideas for articles on your publication's general topic—they'll be those splashy headlines on the cover meant to lure readers.

How will you do that? The same as editors everywhere do. You'll look at what everyone else around you, and around your clients, is writing and talking about. It's this month's "Topic A" in your market's world. You'll write about it too—but adding your own special take on the subject. And you'll link whatever Topic

A is this month, to your SME. Believe it or not, Topic A is often as elementary as the weather or the time of year. Think how the fitness magazines tell you how to stay in shape through the tough winter, then how to slim down for summer. Well, if your profession is to help people maintain financial fitness, your magazine cover lines follow the same approach: how to generate tax savings at year's end... how to line up the bucks for Junior's college tuition payments...

It's early December as I write this, and I've just read a prominently displayed article in one of the world's leading newspapers, the *Wall Street Journal*, on how to stay sober and out of trouble at the office Christmas party. It's thorough, complete, and well-written. I'd give the reporter an "A," and I'd never get in hot water at any party if I followed his advice. It's just that this exact same article could have been, and probably was, written last year, the year before, and the year before that—maybe even in the *Wall Street Journal*. And you can be sure you'll be reading that article somewhere next holiday season too, and it will contain pretty much the same exact common-sense tips.

But while you or I might pass up this information—hey, we know that already—someone else doesn't know that already: The European expatriate here for a year on a work visa and unfamiliar with American work protocols. The twenty-two-year-old straight out of college three months into her first corporate job. And someone else welcomes the same advice as a refresher course: the rising junior VP whose career stumbled after *he* stumbled out the door a little too tipsy at last year's party.

The top publications and TV shows repeat the same topics all the time—they just find a reason to link it to something that's *now.* That's why I urge you not to sweat over selecting your topics. It's OK—even good—for the same ones to come up again and again. And you don't need much of a connection between your subject and the calendar, or the news, to come up with twelve messages a year.

So here's your twelve-item marketing calendar for the year: Your four SMEs, twice a year each. One time it's a seasonal connection, the second time it's something timely—linked to something in the news or on everyone's mind, like when the state legislature passes a bill that affects your clients. Four times two; that's eight connections. For number nine go back to some profound thought you once had while writing those first eight, but that you cut out because it was too long. Dust it off. Three to go: Quick thoughts on two random matters that catch your attention at some point in the year… and then a personal year-end holiday message. And now you're done: twelve connections with your marketplace, one a month.

Now you've got to make it easy to get done. Your goal: come up with just a handful of sentences—as many words as you can squeeze out in twenty minutes (or as many of a colleague/subordinate/outsourced vendor's words, if they will be writing for you, as you can review and polish in twenty minutes. I'll go into more detail shortly about how to make this part happen.) What are the two or three things you'd tell someone in an elevator between the nineteenth floor and the lobby about the topic you've chosen? Can you put together three sentences on your key topics with some help, if need be, from a colleague or subordinate? Yes, you can. You do it every time you talk to a client or even a prospect.

Creating your marketing message with the mPOWER system is reasonably quick and painless. It does require some effort—but far less than what most professionals struggle with when they try to create traditional marketing stuff. To illustrate, imagine you are a professional residential lawn and garden care service and it's time for your spring mailing. In the left column are the rules to follow in creating a simple piece. On the right, you'll see how your gardening service can follow them to create a simple marketing piece. (Since I'm profoundly ignorant on this topic, apologies if my example falls short of 100 percent accuracy.)

1. State the broad topic and the reason your audience should care about it right now.

"Spring's almost here—time for your lawn and garden to wake up!"

2. Offer 3-4 tips about it—in simple list or tidbit format, not in lengthy sentences.

"Here's how to start the season: Clear out last fall's leftover leaves.

Find the bulbs your dog dug up over the winter, and stick them back in the earth.

Trim the overgrowth you didn't get to last December."

3. The call to action: Confirm that your reader may want to know more, and set yourself up as the resource to go to— WITHOUT hard-sell.

"For a free, no-obligation article with twenty more practical, time-saving tips, visit our web site: www.GardensRUs. com/tips/spring."

4. Now, OFFER but do not PUSH yourself as an additional resource.

Or, "call Holly or Fern at 777-555-1234 for more complimentary advice."

5. Close with all contact info. and a slogan; in e-mail, include a "signature" you create once and always use.

"Keep Your Lawns Green and Your Hands Clean"

Gardens R Us, 777-555-1234 1212 Thornberry Road Fertile, MN 50010 www.GardensRUs.com e-mail: Rose@GardensRUs.com

---

For an expanded, printable version of this chart, visit **www.MediaImpact.biz/resources/how-to**

OK, I know most folks reading this book are likely to be engaged in professions and occupations that deal with more abstract knowledge and skills. You may be wondering, "How does this apply to me?" So if that's you, here are another few examples.

You're an investment and financial strategies adviser. It's early December.

Your message:

> *Another year is drawing to a close. There's still time to pursue some strategies that may reduce this year's tax obligations come next April 15. For many people, these timely moves may make sense:*
>
> 1. *Sell some of your money-losing assets to create a loss that will offset your year's income. Reinvest in similar investment vehicles, or—after thirty days pass—right back into the same asset.*
>
> 2. *Pre-pay your January mortgage payment before December 31 to receive the interest deduction this year.*
>
> 3. *Accelerate payments on any pending charitable contributions or medical bills to this year.*
>
> *To learn more about these and seventeen more strategies, visit our resource corner at www.YourDollars4U.com for a longer article. Of course, everyone's situation is different, so you can also call us, no obligation, at 888-555-9876.*
>
> *Season's Greetings.*
>
> *Scrimpp & Save, Chartered Financial Advisers*
>
> *"Protecting Financial Futures for Three Generations of Virginians"*
>
> *www.YourDollars4U.com*
> *e-mail: info@YourDollars4U.com*
>
> *888-555-9876*
> *Fax: 888-555-6789*

You're a trusts and estates lawyer. Let's say Congress has just repealed the estate tax, and this has been reported widely in the general news media. Your message:

> *Repeal of the estate tax is an historic change that affects thousands of people in our area. If your net worth exceeds $2 million you face important decisions, and you may have to take some actions soon:*

- *Your will may need to be modified*
- *You may want to consider changes in your investment portfolio*
- *You should review the beneficiaries of your investment accounts.*

I have prepared some additional information in a brief article, and you may either access it for no cost at www.TRustlaw.com, request it by e-mailing info@TRustlaw.com, or call my office at 866-555-2345 and ask to have it mailed or faxed.

Protect Your Assets to Protect Your Heirs

T. Rust & Esta Tess, attorneys at law

www.TRustlaw.com

866-555-2345

Fax: 866-555-7654

e-mail: T.Rust@TRustlaw.com

You're a time management consultant, and it's late May:

Summer's coming, with its relaxing weekends and perhaps a vacation at the shore. But for many of us, remaining focused and productive at work becomes a greater challenge this time of year. Here are some strategies that may help you:

- *Each Monday morning, identify the week's three biggest priorities and block out time for them, as if they were scheduled meetings.*
- *Learn well in advance when key clients, colleagues, and contacts will go on vacation, so you can complete any essential work with them before they go.*
- *Discipline yourself to read and send e-mail messages only at three or four points in the day, not constantly as they arrive.*

I've worked with hundreds of busy people over the years, and I've developed many time management strategies by observing them. To see my list of 100 time management do's and don'ts, visit my website

at www.TimeMan.com or request it by e-mailing
info@TimeMan.com.

"Favor the Moment"
Dewitt Daley, the Time Management Pro
www.TimeMan.com
866-555-5432
Fax: 866-555-6789
e-mail:D.Daley@TimeMan.com

And that's about it, four parts:

- Intro or urgency-establisher
- Three to four tips
- Call to action
- Signature and contact info

Don't race through the last step, by the way. Coming up with a signature phrase is well worth your time and thought—it's the kind of thing that sticks in peoples' minds. Focus, in creating yours, on the benefits and results that clients get from working with you. Keep the same one permanently, or change it seasonally to fit different occasions. I love the one an excellent freelance business writer I know, Maerwydd McFarland, tacked on to her year-end Season's Greetings e-mail:

"May the New Year find you never at a loss for words."

Now let's explore the options for deciding who writes these little pieces—you, a colleague, an employee, or a vendor you hire. First ask yourself: Can I do something like this once a month? Will I? As a successful professional, you already have the subject matter knowledge you need for this task. But not everyone can, or wants to, sit down at the keyboard and write even this little bit of a marketing message. Some of us don't have the time. Or the interest. Or the confidence. In my experience, about one in three professional people have the aptitude and inclination to write like this. If you're one of the other two, you have options. You simply have to find an easy, inexpensive way to get someone who's among the one in three to help you. You'll provide the info and subject matter expertise, and they'll put what you know into written form. Fortunately, that is very do-able, as you'll see in the next pages.

Some professionals in business initially resist the notion of getting help. I've never understood why. These same people invite total strangers into their homes to clean them, deposit their $45,000 motor vehicle at repair shops where young men they've never met will tinker with its innards, and expose the intimate details of their physique to the tailor who'll fit their brand new cocktail dress. What's the big deal about getting help with a job that's outside your core expertise, or that isn't the best use of your time? We all do it all the time.

Now, some great news: unlike these other delegated chores, half the time you don't even have to pay for help with writing your marketing messages. (And when you do, it'll usually cost less than tuning up that Lexus). Here's how:

Option 1: Ask a colleague or peer. If you have a partner, chances are you already divide up responsibilities and chores. Have the best writer on your team handle this one.

Option 2: Ask an employee. Admins, interns, clerical assistants, and other non-professionals on your team have skills you may never see. In even the smallest organizations, there's usually one person on staff who can write—and wants to. Put them to work.

Option 3: Ask a relative, neighbor, or friend. Just as in option 2, there's usually someone in this crowd who's adept with words—and who either owes you a favor, or is open to helping you in a friendly barter arrangement.

Option 4: Buy a couple hours of a freelance writer's time. Business writers are not terribly expensive, as a rule. How to find one? Look on Craigslist, Mediabistro, elance.com, freelancewriting.com, or a similar online listing. Ask colleagues and acquaintances for recommendations. Check your area's local chapter of the American Society of Journalists and Authors (asja.org), International Association of Business Communicators (iabc.com), or Public Relations Society of America (prsa.org). Inquire at the local university. Call your town's Chamber of Commerce or Kiwanis. Call your local community college or university for an English major or journalist student.

Wait, I hear you silently screaming. *These people don't know my subject area! They can't do this for me!*

Yes, they can. They do it every day for professionals just like you. Here's how easy it is:

You've already identified your topic, and you have a pretty good amount of knowledge about it. Having identified your writer, reserve about twenty minutes of face time or phone time with him or her. Not one minute more! That would be a waste of time. In that time, you talk. They listen and take notes. You'll just talk on the topic, without thinking of how it will look in print. Most people who don't write find it easy to talk. Next step: the writer leaves. You return to serving your clients. And in a day or two, the writer presents you with a brief article or message—whatever you've told them to do. You invest another five or ten minutes to edit, polish, and correct any factual errors in their work. You're now done. (If you find you're devoting more than five to ten minutes to the editing task, find yourself a better writer, or one who listens more intently.)

Alternatively, some people find it easier to take keyboard in hand and crank out a first draft themselves. They don't worry about style, or readability, or length. They just get it all out of them. Then, they turn it over to that same freelance writer, or one with special editing strengths, who turns it into beautiful, succinct prose.

You may have already written something longer for your professional society, or for a client presentation, or a speech. But it's way too long and detailed for marketing purposes. So, just hand it over to your writer, who will chop it down to size and make it sing.

Either method works—and neither costs as much as the old-school technique of creating and buying an ad.

8

14 SIMPLE STRATEGIES TO ATTRACT PROSPECTS

Next up, let's turn these little gems of writing into marketing pieces, and get them in front of the eyeballs of your prospects and sustainers—and anyone else important who's on your list.

Two chapters back, I promised you a way to market on zero dollars a month. That's the first strategy: **e-mail.** It's so important it gets its own chapter in this book, right after this one. For now, know that all it takes, if you wish to keep it simple, is to send your little message in one e-mail blast, once a month, to your whole list. No fancy graphics, attachments, or gimmicks, just a few quick words and done with it. Now, get back to servicing the clients.

But if you're ready for the advanced course, let's add some angles. E-mail is great, but it's not the only game in town. Everybody in the marketplace responds differently to the modern panoply of communications media. Some people swear by e-mail; others eschew it. Some businesspeople look forward to catching up on their snail mail on the train or plane; others toss it with alacrity. And there's more. My friend Mike underscored for me how much more. Whenever we'd get together to talk about marketing, he'd get so excited about some of the concepts I was sharing that I'd recommend some books on the topic. That's when his face would sag: "Ned, I just can't get myself to read. I'm a listening type—I want it on a disc I can stick into my car player for the drive home."

Mike was my reminder that no one marketing medium is the right one. It really is different strokes for different folks. Most people like to listen to music, for example. But we all have our preferred delivery system: radio, Walkman, iPod, MP3, CD player, and more. Same with receptivity to marketing messages: I'll hang up on any salesperson who calls me; I'll toss 99 percent of the junk mail I get. But I'll open at least two unsolicited e-mails a day.

E-mail remains the medium of choice for small professional practices and businesspeople to market: it's inexpensive, and easy to do. But since it's impossible to guess what works best for whom, the smart move is to mix it up in your marketing.

Snail Mail: Three or four times a year, put your marketing message into letter form on paper, and stick it in an envelope.

Fax: Remember the fax machine? Now that it's out of favor, people tend to notice again when it spits out a fax. Try this method, too, once a year or so. More, if you discover it works for you.

Postcards: I love postcards as an expertise marketing tool. They are fun, inexpensive, and really easy. They are an excellent way to fill all or part of your yearly quota of mailed pieces. That's because sending a letter, as I described above, can set people onto the counterproductive sidetrack of trying to write too much, despite my exhortations. All that white space on a page tempts them, and pretty soon they're bogged down in too much effort and unnecessary detail. Here's how you do postcards instead: go online to find one of the many excellent suppliers who produce attention-grabbing postcards. No need to have your own ones designed unless you have the budget: these suppliers have vast stocks of visually appealing, eye-catching, and even humorous styles to choose from. Buy one with a front picture or design that appeals to you, and have that supplier or one in your town custom-print the back for you. On the back you'll print the same length and type message you'd send in an e-mail. Follow the same five-step message assembly guide I covered a few pages back. Slap a mailing label and postcard stamp on, and you're done. Better yet: write your message to relate to the front-side visual. For instance, your front side has an adorable photo of some cute babies. Your rear-side message: "Selling your house isn't child's play. Five tips on how to maximize your home's resale value." Who's gonna get a cutie-pie baby picture postcard and not take at least a peek at the reverse side?

Advertising: Still hooked on advertising in the local paper or the trade press? Instead of your usual "Happy Holidays from your family dentist Jen Jones" ad, buy the same space—but fill it with three tips on dental hygiene.

Web site: Once in a while, post your little article on your web site instead of in an e-mail. Then use your bulk e-mail list to send out a one-line headline with a link to the site, telling people to go there for the information. You've now connected with the attention-short-but-love-to-browse-the-web crowd. (Plenty more about your web site coming up in the pages ahead.)

The Internet: This too is so important, and simultaneously so much bigger yet easier to master, that it gets its own chapter. Right after the next one. (Hint: your own web site is just a small piece of the Internet strategy.)

The e-newsletter or e-zine: A somewhat slicked-up version of e-mail marketing, this is so easy and so effective, I can't understand why everyone doesn't do one. Reliable, low-cost vendors like ConstantContact.com make it look snappy, and take virtually all the hassles and tech headaches out of the process. The trick is to keep it simple and short. You design it once, using an elementary setup template. Then, once a month or however often you wish, you toss together a couple of paragraphs of advice or information (the same as you do for your e-mail and mail messages) and if you'd like, add a few tidbits of anything else you feel like saying that month. Like everything else I discuss in this book, resist the temptation to shill your wares and be embarrassingly self-promotional. Stick to being *useful* and people will open your e-mails.

Audio CDs: For people like my friend Mike, you sometimes should talk instead of write. With today's basic technology, it's now possible to sit at your desk and *record* your words of advice rather than write them down. Just speak conversationally, and remember to inflect and vary your voice tone. Practice this by first listening to the pros on radio do it. In this format, you'll probably want to go longer, with more depth and detail, than in your brief written pieces. But here too, use cocktail party chit-chat as your marker: keep it brief, basic, and interesting. You're not offering comprehensive education on your topic; you're hitting the high points. When your piece is recorded, burn it onto CDs and mail them out to your list with a cover note. If this is beyond your technological abilities, the nearest computer geek can do this for you in his sleep.

My mentor and friend Mark LeBlanc, a remarkably incisive expert on growing a small business, is one of many who have taken this format to a higher level. An extremely polished professional speaker—good enough to be president of the National Speakers Association—Mark knows that in an audio format, even the best speaker can start to sound too much like a talking head if the recording goes on too long. So Mark headed into a recording studio with a freelance interviewer he hired for the day, and gave the interviewer a suggested list of questions to fire at him. The result: a lively CD that mimics the familiar talk-radio interview format we all know so well. Mark's delivery comes across as fresh, original, and entertaining—which it is—in this format.

Audio file: Once in a while, take the same recording and, rather than burn it onto a disk, save it as an electronic file you can e-mail or post on your web site. Now, the technophiles on your list can download it to their portable audio devices, or just listen straight from their computers.

Self-published articles: Another variation on the mailing piece: It's amazingly simple, using basic software your high-schooler at home can operate better than you, to create a dynamic-looking one-page article that looks as if it stepped from the pages of *Business Week* or *Fortune*. You just create a simple template once, complete with your photo or any other graphic you choose, then paste a word-processed file into it. In seconds you have turned what might have been a boring two-page marketing letter—the kind no one ever reads—into a single colorful, attractive, and readable page that looks like a magazine reprint. It gets much more attention and reaction than that typical letter mailing. Bonus technique: once in a while turn it into a pdf file, and e-mail it to your list in place of the regular monthly message.

> *Want a handy sheet of guidelines to help you write a basic article? I've got one at* **www. MediaImpact.biz/resources/article.**

Blogs *and* **podcasts:** As I write, these are the two hottest delivery methods spreading through the business world. Next year, it'll be something else, and these will simply be two of the standard tools in your arsenal. Stay in touch with what's new on the horizon in technology! Once these methods reach critical mass of usage, as blogs and podcasts now have, two things happen: they become easier to use, because someone has figured out a simple way to put their power into your hands; and they become cheaper, because they've entered the mass market. My advice: most of us non-techie professionals don't need to be first on our block to jump on a new bandwagon. The effort and the cost are usually still too high when these methodologies are new. But as soon as they are on the cusp of being mainstream, that's when to jump on board. How to know when the time is right? Two cues: when you start using them as a consumer, because giant companies have deployed them—and about six months after your kids are doing them.

Blogs and podcasts, at this writing, fit that category. Consider them if you can fit in just a couple of hours more per month. Blogs are basically an online home for you to showcase your thoughts and words on your SME topics. It's nothing more complicated than a running journal or commentary, which you can post to as often or infrequently, as in-depth or as surface as you want. Most blogs are set up to allow readers to post their own reactions to what you've said, and their own comments. That's called interactivity, and it's great because when the audience is engaged, they're more likely to return frequently to catch up on who's saying what. (And hopefully develop a virtual relationship with you.) The technology to do this, by the way, is now accessible, inexpensive, and easy for any of us computer-challenged people to do. You can get started literally in minutes. Here's how: You search for, or ask peers or the computer geeks in your life, for a service that creates and runs blogs for people like us. There are several, and the cost runs from nothing to minimal. You set yourself up, and you start writing.

A podcast is basically your own personal radio station. Its audience is your database—those people, at least, who tell you they want to receive little snippets of your thoughts and advice in audio form, to hear via their iPod or computer, every so often. I'll discuss these further in the Internet marketing chapter.

Best Blogging

Has anybody had any successes or interesting results in blogging or podcasting to market to prospects? Share your story with me, and I'll post it or publish it for others to see and learn from. Send it to me at info@Mediaimpact.biz.

Speaking: This tactic could cover a whole chapter by itself. I'll simplify here: Speaking to groups is an unstoppable way to attract new clients. Just make sure it's a group that matches your target market. Skip the truck drivers' association annual meeting if your clients are retail jewelers. When you identify the right group, offer to speak for free at an upcoming meeting. When they agree, make the most of it and maximize your impact. Announce your pending speaking engagement on your web site and in a press release. Spread the word to your marketing database with an e-mail blast; regardless of whether they can attend, they will be impressed that you have been invited—you must be *the* expert, they'll conclude. Ask the sponsoring organization if they'll publicize your talk, and offer to write an article on your topic for their publication. Ask them if they will audio or video tape your presentation; if so, request a copy, and you'll have another product for future marketing purposes, perhaps even to offer for sale.

Then go and give a great speech. Follow the same mPOWER system you've learned to serve up some expertise-marketing. No hard sell or product promotion—your sponsoring group won't allow that anyway. Just stick to the information, knowledge, and wisdom you know this audience needs. Mix in some funny but instructive stories. Drop some indirect references to how much further you benefit paying clients, as in "Those are the high points of how to market by public speaking. There are more techniques that I share with my clients, which we don't have time for today, but I've just given you the best of it." At some point in your presentation, invite people to give you their business card afterwards, if they want to learn more. Hold back some valuable details from your speech—you can't cover everything in the brief time allotted to you—and invite your audience to access this bonus information on your web site, where you've conveniently posted it for them. (I usually put my entire presentation in a pdf file on the web site, with some extras included, the day before my presentation. I tell my audience they don't have to take extensive notes because they can print out the whole thing when they return to their offices.) After my speech, if I think I've touched on something new or different in it, I might turn my remarks into a press release or article, and distribute it or get it published.

The key takeaway from these fourteen strategies is to keep mixing and keep experimenting. It won't work if it's done once, and it works better when you mix delivery formats. The corollary to this, of course, is—Don't wait. Yes, you'll have some new informational material next month. And maybe some more time next Spring. So what? Do something *now*!

Early one fine morning before delivering a speech in Florida, I went for a jog on the nearly deserted beach. Along the way, I spotted a gorgeous, intact seashell—one I knew would make a nice souvenir for the family back home. Looking around, I saw not a human in sight. "I'll pick it up on the way back—why carry it around with me now?" I told myself.

"EDUCATION SELLS"

Mike Meyers, a Westchester, New York, pension and insurance whiz, is affable, extroverted, and comfortably adept in networking to gain business. But he's come to learn that it's what you say when you get the meeting that matters, not how many meetings you get. He now shuns the sales call. Instead he goes on the "information call."

"Education is what sells today, not product," Mike explains.

Mike's preferred way to build meaningful relationships with prospects is to hold seminars for them. His business lies in helping accounting firms devise tax-saving pension plans for their clients. So whenever he can, he'll go into a C.P.A. firm and present a lecture on the topic for the partners—for no cost and at no obligation.

As often as not, he reports, they end up seeing possibilities they hadn't recognized before, and pretty soon he finds himself working with them as his new client.

Seminars are effective, he says, because C.P.A.s can't possibly keep up with the fast-paced environment of pension law. They welcome the opportunity to learn from someone more expert and up-to-date on this specific niche. While they don't start out expecting to become clients, it happens naturally in the process that unfolds when Mike starts sharing his knowledge.

Mike lets his expertise stand up and be seen. That way, he doesn't have to resort to sales-talk language. He's no longer selling, and the prospect is no longer buying. He's sharing and teaching—and they're deciding that working with him just makes good business sense.

You know the next part. Did I forget the spot where I had seen it? Did the tide carry it away or bury it? Doesn't matter. It was gone. Opportunities exist in the present. Seize them. Don't waste time worrying about which technique or medium to use—just pick one and get started. I'm amused at the endless discussion among professional marketers over which format or medium works "best." The answer, as we've seen here, is that there's no one answer—it really is different strokes.

And while I'm on the subject: Don't get hung up either in the self-imposed pressure to do everything, to do one of each technique. Save your energy for something important, like taking an occasional afternoon off to play with your family. At the moment (it often changes) my entire marketing campaign consists of just three moves:

- I send out my e-newsletter once a month, religiously, to anyone who wants it. (And I never let it take me more than one hour, top to bottom.)
- I write several articles a year, which are posted on and distributed by Internet publications that target the same markets I do.
- I stay in touch, one way or another—in person, by phone, by mail, or virtually—with the people I consider my biggest fans, and the short list of my sustainers.

Actually, there's a fourth component most months: I make it my business to check in for guidance and wisdom from the smartest guy I know on the subject of business growth for a small organization. His name—I've mentioned him before—is Mark LeBlanc. I learned the strategy from him of contacting my biggest fans—he calls them *advocates*—regularly, and many more razor-sharp strategies. If you're interested in Mark's take on business growth, you can check out www.SmallBusinessSuccess.com.

9
YOU'RE NOT SPAM

E-mail is so crucial to marketing for small, solo, and midsized professional practices and organizations that it earns its own chapter here.

As I've said, e-mail is probably the best single way to go for those of us in this crowd—certainly for anyone who wants this whole marketing business to be easy, quick, low-cost, and effective. Most of us should make it the backbone of our overall business development efforts—with at least six short messages a year to our target list, and more if we're not doing the other stuff just outlined in the chapter before this.

But jumping into some e-mail how-to's and what-to's, let's get a grip on the big what-not-to.

In e-mail land, that's the *p-word*. Permission. As in people on your list granting you permission to send them your e-mails. Because you are in the professional services and want the public to see you as the trusted resource you really are, you have to be ethical and responsible in your marketing. Don't add people to your list without getting their OK.

This isn't as daunting as it sounds. When I meet people, whether one-on-one or when I speak to groups, I'll say something like, "Give me your card if you want to see some more common-sense marketing suggestions once in a while," or "If you'd like to follow what I'm working on and thinking about, give me your card and we can stay in touch." Anyone who signs up for my e-newsletter online automatically sees a privacy statement and a way to get off my list (unsubscribe) should they ever want to.

Always let people know they have the choice to opt out at any time. (To see what my procedure looks like, click on any page on my web site www.MediaImpact.biz and fill in the sign-up blank). It's rare for a subscriber to drop out, but if they ever wake up one morning and decide I'm useless to them, they are free to say good-bye.

None of this takes more than a minute for you to do. You do it just once when you set things up initially if you use a service like Constant Contact, as I currently do. This online service handles all the work for you—including, if you want, all the administrative chores of managing your list. The cost is peanuts.

Are you a spammer if you send out a few hundred, or even a few thousand messages to the world? Not if they have invited you to stay in touch. When you have obtained permission, your words fall on receptive ears and eyes. You may remember that I assured you earlier you'd be connecting exclusively with an audience of people who already know you, and like you. That's much more effective than opening your window and shouting down to a bunch of strangers.

Please—unless you've got the money to invest and staff resources to help you, or you run a large operation serving a significant number of clients/patients/customers, don't buy lists of names. When you do, you're reduced to the equivalent of cold-calling. Whether e-mail or street addresses, your odds of success are reduced accordingly. A better investment: use your resources to improve, increase, and enhance your outreach to the people already in your database. Or, when you're truly eager to advance to the next level, invest strategically not in lists and blind direct mail—but in some carefully targeted PR. Carefully targeted publicity, in my experience, can lift a small practice or organization to new heights much more cost-effectively.

Back to this issue of spam, for a moment. Even though you're not spam, will some people treat you as if you are? Will whole bunches of people on your list pass your message by and hit the delete key? Sure. That's inevitable—a reality of marketing. Just as the best baseball players are still out seven times out of ten. But you're going to do better than most marketers, because your audience is primed to expect something of potential interest and use from you—not the usual marketing drivel. Recent research I've seen concludes that people open e-mails from companies they trust, and that the way to win that trust is to be user-focused, with useful information.

More important: even those who delete you (and by the way, the entire Internet marketing industry thrives despite the reality that 96 percent of people will delete) will see your name and your message's subject line before they hit that nasty little key. You've scored an impression; you're on their radar screen for another month. This, too, qualifies as Mission Accomplished. Remember—they already know and value you. The impression you leave when they eyeball your name for a second actually means something—it amounts to more than the one that forms from messages about a box of cereal or even a new sports car.

Your only real worry with e-mail is a good problem to have: Your list grows and grows; you have a few thousand names, and spam filters start blocking you out. You'll know when this happens because you will get some bounce-backs, and the colleagues, relatives, and friends you'll keep on your list as a control will inform you of the problem. Should this occur, you'll simply break your list into smaller pieces, and send it out in four or five blasts, instead of all at once. Problem solved.

If you've been paying attention, you noticed that two paragraphs above, I referred to the subject line in your e-mail. That's really important. Make that *critical*.

What you say in five or six words in the subject line matters more than everything else you say—combined.

It's what people notice. (Sometimes, it's all they notice—remember all those folks who are going to delete you, but can't help read your subject line before they do?) It either draws them in, or sends them away. It either interests, intrigues, or piques them or it sends them away. So, make it good.

"December newsletter from David Dentist" won't do. How about "Don't Let Tooth Decay Wreck Your Holidays, by David Dentist"?

"News from Allison Accountant" tells the reader nothing. "Ten tax-saving tips from Allison Accountant" does more. Make sure your subject lines contain your name and a few really snappy, creative words. Here's one place where it's OK and fun to be creative—even if you're a lawyer! Did your state just pass some onerous new insurance requirement that's going to affect boaters? Try "New Maritime Law Need Not Sink Sailors."

The second most important part of your e-mail is the first sentence, or lead. Keep it simple. Keep it very short. Make it clever. Avoid the long, cumbersome phrases, the kind that can leave you wondering—if you know what I mean in this context—exactly where the sentence started, and precisely what the point of it was in the first place, assuming it had one, regardless of whether it covered something the reader cares about strongly.

See what I mean?

Count words. I'm serious. When I was a rookie newspaper reporter brimming with more enthusiasm than talent, I ran up against an editor who would reject any story whose first paragraph contained more than twenty-five words. For twenty months, I cursed him nightly. But for the next twenty years, I silently thanked him.

The entire first paragraph of an e-mail should be just two or three sentences maximum (and one is fine). It needs to be really clear, dead on the point, and well written. When I was a PR executive and clients would ask whether I'd finished writing their promised press release, I'd tell them, "I'm almost done. I've written the headline and the first sentence."

Again, I was being serious. If I learned one worthwhile gem from my days in journalism and PR, it's that the headline and the lead are 90 percent of the game. You have one chance to snare the attention of a busy prospect or reader. If they like what they see up on the top, you'll have them for the rest of the ride, too.

Devote ample time to your lead sentence and paragraph, just as you do with your subject line. The rest of your message does not need to be as adroitly crafted; it can just be straightforward informational. As long as you keep *all* of those sentences short.

"I know how to get attention," some clever people inevitably think. "I'll put in some catchy graphics, maybe even with animation."

Great. Now you look just like a Chevrolet ad. Plus, you run the risk that some corporate systems, and some home-based computers, may bounce your message because they don't let all that gimcrackery past the gate. Keep it simple. The days when you could invade someone's brain by flashing some animation are long gone. Once I showed my son Ben what was at the time a marvel: on the Internet, an accurate image of that day's *New York Times* front page. In the middle was a photo of a sailboat. I was quite amazed at what technology had wrought. Ben saw things differently, and he burst my bubble in an instant. "That's nice, Daddy," he said. "Now click on the boat and make it move." Ben was five at the time, which was the late 1990s. Get over the idea that you're going to excite any awake adult with visual stuff. It is now taken for granted, part of the background. In my monthly e-newsletter, I limit visuals to bare necessities. And sometimes I'll just send a text-only, graphics-free message.

Also good to avoid in your e-mails: attachments. Some recipients' systems will simply reject them; some recipients will perform the rejection personally by not opening them, due to indifference or inability. If you have something in a Word file you want your audience to see, cut and paste it into the e-mail text. If it contains graphics or it is a pdf file, this may be the time for that occasional faxed marketing message I suggested a couple of chapters back.

What else to avoid in e-mails? The word "free." (Spam filters may block you at the gate.) Long-winded, unfocused, chatty messages… Advice and information that isn't really informative or newsworthy… Anything about your company picnic. (*"Oh look, Stephanie, these folks had such a good time playing softball at their picnic. Let's hire them to manage our investment portfolio."*)

Just remember this e-mail formula:

- a snappy subject line
- a great opening sentence
- a few bullet points of a sentence or two, max
- a meaningful signature phrase at the bottom

… and you're done.

Listen one more time: An e-mail message needs to be simple. Its job is to *connect* with the prospect, not to close the deal. Its methodology, in the mPOWER scheme, is to showcase you, not to provide an advanced education. It's a spark, not a comprehensive lesson on your subject matter.

Let's close with some further thoughts about the e-newsletter tactic I touched on in the last chapter. My e-newsletter always follows the same format: Two extremely brief nuggets of advice. My business logo, my photo, and a few words about me in the caption under it. A few low-key words about some special service or product I'm offering, perhaps a link to another resource I'm recommending. Then—just for the fun of it–an amazing true fact about something, a thought-provoking quote I've seen recently, and a joke or cartoon. While these latter items often align loosely with my overall theme of expertise marketing, they are really just there for entertainment. People have told me they open my e-newsletters just for the joke. That's fine with me—I'm implanting myself and my service in their minds along the way. (To see my e-newsletter, go to www.MediaImpact.biz and click on any page for quick sign-up.)

Once you truly understand how e-mail marketing works for professionals, using it becomes easy.

> *E-mail marketing do's and don'ts: for a one-page tip sheet summing it all up, visit* **www.MediaImpact.biz/resources/email.**

10

HAVING A WEB SITE IS NOT AN INTERNET STRATEGY

Having a good web site is not an Internet strategy.

That's Rule # 2 of Internet marketing for smaller-sized practices and organizations.

Rule # 1, you may have guessed, is to have a good web site. It's just that when you do, you're not yet an effective marketer on the net. You've simply taken the first, critical step.

Please note, by the way: I did not say have a *great* web site. To attract clients and stimulate referrals, *good* will suffice. *You* are who needs to be great—in client service and in sharpening your mPOWER approach to expertise marketing to get the phone ringing.

Let's dispense quickly with the trap that I still see some organizations fall into: the "My clients aren't on the Internet" trap. Yes, they are. Or they will be in a few months, or next year. And if not, they're either not long for this world—or not a client you really want, anyway.

Having dispensed with that one, let's dive into Rules #1 and #2. Together they are the elements of smart Internet marketing for the likes of businesspeople like us. As you might suspect, that means different from Internet marketing for MTV, or Microsoft, or Kraft Foods, or 99 percent of what we see and think of as good Internet marketing. (That's because *we*, as independent professionals in our own business, are different from 99 percent of the business world.)

Smart Internet marketing, to me, means do-able yet effective. Let's start with your own web site (see Rule # 1) and then explore the other fourteen billion pages on the World Wide Web (see Rule # 2), to see how you can put some of them to work prospecting business for you.

If you've been with me this far, you know what's coming:

Your web site is *not* a self-promotional, "look-at-me-I'm-great" bore.

Your web site *is* the place where you showcase your expertise.

Your web site is *not* a brochure transplanted into cyberspace.

Your web site *is* where you attract prospects, sustainers, and leads to develop and enhance a virtual relationship with you, where they learn to value, respect, and need your expertise and sound judgment.

Your web site is a resource for these people. It gives them what they want and need, on a regular basis. It contains tips, advice, information, and simple articles.

It makes them want—maybe even *need*—to come back regularly.

Your web site doesn't get done once, and then you call it finished. It is dynamic, changing frequently with the addition of new content and information.

Your web site doesn't cost you a lot of money to create or design, and it doesn't take a lot of time, cash, energy, or work to increase its value by updating and expanding it often.

Your web site's job is not to close the sale. It's simply to advance your virtual relationships with prospects. Your site just needs to get them interested enough that, when they are ready and have concluded it might be the right fit, they'll call you.

Your web site brings those people back regularly, because they're used to finding timely new content, and more useful information, when they return.

Your web site is the hub and nerve center of your entire marketing/business development machinery: It's where you first send the people you meet to learn more about you…. It's where you sign them up to subscribe to your e-newsletter, your periodic e-mail messages, or your direct mail pieces…. It's where you post the extra, enriched materials that you offer to readers of your e-mailings…. It's where people learn how to contact you directly…. It's where people who read your articles elsewhere on the Web (which they'll start doing soon after you read the next section) land when they click on the "learn more" button.

It's where you give them news they need to know about your SME before they find out about it somewhere else, or—if it's already been in the news—where you give them the expert interpretation and analysis they can't get anyplace else.

It's where you tell your audience that you'll be speaking on your topic next month at the Chamber of Commerce breakfast, and where you'll post your presentation and notes after the speech.

None of this, I'm glad to say, is particularly complicated or expensive to do.

All it takes is to gather up those little messages you've been writing for your e-mail and other marketing, and get them onto the site. If you're feeling ambitious, go ahead and expand some of those brief messages into a slightly longer form—but promise me you'll stop at three hundred to four hundred words, max! (If someone's doing the writing for you, ask them if they can take the information you've already downloaded verbally to them and turn it into some new pieces.)

If you have someone maintaining your web site for you, just give them all this stuff and ask them to find a good way to add it to the site. They'll know how. If you manage your own web site, you'll want to create a new page or section that you call "resources," "articles," "useful info," or some such broad title. Put everything in that section for now. Later on, when your little online library gets overcrowded, you can break it out into sections based on subject matter.

While you're talking with your web person, ask him/her to join you in a little brainstorming exercise: If you wanted to turn your site into a one-stop resource center for everything critical that your clients and prospects need to know, what else would it have? Copies of (or links to) important government forms? Reprints of timely news articles on topics that vitally affect your client base? Reprints of publicity about *you*? That paper you presented to your professional organization last summer? Links to associations and organizations they should know about?

There are two reasons to fill out your web site with enrichment like this. As prospects and other visitors catch on that they can get everything they need from your site, they're likely to visit it more often. The virtual relationship with them deepens, and more of them become clients sooner. And the more material you add to your site, and especially the more links to *other* web sites, the higher your ranking on Google and other search engines. This, as you'll see in a few pages, is really crucial to enlarging your universe of leads and prospects.

So—save all that money others are spending on flashy, expensive web design and gimmickry. Invest a fraction of that amount on adding substance to your site. In your world, unlike the consumer products marketing game, it's what the customer values.

As you can see, your web site is a pretty important, and very busy, place. But you're not an artist. You haven't created your site to simply sit there and look pretty. You've created it to do a job for you—to attract visitors and start building your virtual relationship with them. Your high quality, no-nonsense, no-blatant-self-promotion web approach will win visitors over, but how do you get them there in the first place? Broadly, there are three ways:

- You'll tell them to go there.
- They'll find you while searching the Internet under your topic or SME.
- They'll find your presence, and links to your site, on other web sites they are visiting.

To be effective on the web, you have to get all three happening. The good news is there's no need to learn a new set of skills, or invest massive time or money, to get there. This stuff pretty much takes place on autopilot, once you set a few moves in motion—all which will sound familiar, since they're mPOWER strategies you now understand.

RESOURCE-FUL WEB SITE

 Boulder, Colorado, Realtor Dick Gilbert builds his entire marketing strategy around an information-rich web site for consumers. You'll find no hard sell, and barely anything about Dick himself, at www.dickgilbert.com.

Instead, you'll find five hundred pages of useful knowledge—about buying a home, relocating, and life in Boulder. Dick did it all himself—"It's a home brew job," he says—starting originally on a free web hosting service from AOL.

Visitors from all over the world view his site, and many become buyers—a diplomat from Switzerland among his recent clients. The site is "virtually my only marketing tool," Dick says, having replaced his pre-web strategies of direct marketing and local advertising. It accounts for about two of every three sales—the other deals coming from repeat clients.

Dick created dickgilbert.com to give people more information on his community than they'd find practically anywhere else. In December 2006, when severe winter weather in the area made national headlines, his site clocked one million visits. He must be doing something right: Google gives him top search listings for Boulder real estate. To remain there, he updates his content often, and links to many other sites—three thousand at last count.

It takes Dick about $20 a month, and an hour a day, to run the site. "You can do just as well as the big guys," Dick Gilbert says of his results.

Telling them: You *tell* people to visit your site by putting its address—known to techies as its URL—everywhere you can. On your letterhead. In every communication you send out. On your business cards. When you speak to audiences and chat one-on-one. At the bottom of your published articles, along with your name and biographical information. Anywhere you can, proactively and consistently.

I once walked into a men's room just as the legendary rock concert promoter Sid Bernstein, the man who many years earlier had brought the Beatles to America, was emerging. I knew him only slightly. How, I mused as we exchanged smiles wordlessly, could the unassuming mild-mannered man I occasionally encountered have stood out so brilliantly in the rough-and-tumble, flamboyant world of rock music? I entered the restroom and spotted on the mirrors and along the washbasins three little stickers, touting some upcoming music show, that hadn't been there a couple of hours earlier. Now I understood a little of how Sid did it.

I've known people who could pitch business to the doctors and nurses as they lay on a medical examining table. (Confession: I have done this myself.)

These are two examples of assertiveness in the real world. You need to be similarly creative, consistent, and confident in the new online world—in getting the word out about your web site, and about the benefits of working with you. (Notice, I did not say "about your credentials" or "about how good you are.")

You also have to motivate people to visit your site. (No, they won't go there just because you suggest it, or because they like you. And since you're not Madison Avenue scale, you can't lure them there with fun online video games or giveaways to the World Series.) This gets done, as you now understand, by constantly creating reasons for people to check in. Hence, the resource center approach I just outlined. And since your articles, presentations, and all else you do to market must be brief to succeed, you—and the marketplace—need to send the seriously interested somewhere they can get further details. That somewhere is your web site—as in, "To see a comparison chart that will help you decide which kind of life insurance is right for you, go to my web site." Once you get in the habit of sticking all kinds of useful stuff up there on the site, two things happen: it becomes second nature, so it's no longer a chore, and you become known as the go-to source of information for people who are in the market for what you do.

Old School Marketing: Making flyers or buying ads touting your services.

New School Marketing: Making flyers or buying ads announcing your web site as the place to visit for ten tips on something your target market needs to know.

Think of your web site as a big company's home office, specifically the VP for marketing's office. It's where a lot of the heavy-duty client attraction work gets accomplished. But you also need a sales force out in the field every day, finding, mining, and developing new prospects. That sales force is the rest of the Internet. Here's how you can use it:

Finding you while they search: This second of the three ways to draw visitors to your site is pivotal, but too many professionals think it's such a big job that they couldn't possibly pull it off—so they don't even try. Wrong!

As we all know too well, people—prospective clients—search the Internet every day for information and guidance on your topic of expertise, your SME—perhaps even searching for someone to hire. Unfortunately, they do *not* look by typing your name into the Google box. (If they already knew who you were, they wouldn't be searching.) Instead they enter a few words summarizing your topic.

And why doesn't your name pop up when they do? Sorry, I know you probably think it's because you're the proverbial little guy and some Internet giant, big corporation, or Google advertiser has grabbed the top spot. The truth, my friends, is that you may fail to capture those top search engine rankings for the simple reason that you don't think you can do it—and so you don't even try.

Here's a personal story that may cheer your pessimistic heart: A few years back, I *did* try. At one point, I thought I might want to seek out some public relations business with the financial planning industry. Teaming with a writer friend, I carried out—painlessly and very inexpensively—a plan to position myself for this initiative by raising my rankings in the search engines for this category. (I did not spend a cent on advertising, by the way.)

But then life intruded, as it will. Other distractions and opportunities came along and I ditched my plan. A year or two later, I again entertained thoughts of entering that market with a publicity consulting service. *"Hmmm,"* I wondered. *"What kind of competition is out there?"* I Googled "financial planners + publicity." To my chagrin, six of the first ten listings were for the same person. *"Oh, no,"* I wailed in despair. *"Some guy already owns that space!"*

Then I looked closer. The guy was me. All my previously-published articles were there. And as I write, some eighteen months after the last article I published on that topic, my name *still* pops up number one on Google. It's enough to get you wondering. I never even carried out my original plan of marketing that expertise to that market. I never did anything but submit a bunch of articles following a very specific and targeted strategy. After which I forgot the whole thing.

Imagine what I—or you—could accomplish if we really tried to do something.

Interestingly, you won't see my name anywhere on that number one search engine listing. But the link whisks you to an article—one I posted on someone else's site—with my byline. After you've digested my succinct, 205-word advice and you click on my byline, you get a whole menu of other articles I've written… a link to my web site… and a link to the Amazon.com order form for my first book.

Not bad for not trying, I'd say.

(And by the way, while I'll happily work with financial planners on their marketing and business development, I don't do publicity services per se. Keep *that* in mind next time you think Google has found you the ideal resource match.)

The big idea to remember: When all those Internet searchers look for sound advice, they start with the keywords relating to your topic. So when you go about raising your visibility on the Internet, it can't be visibility for you alone. It *has* to be visibility that starts with your SME topics, but that quickly connects the visitor to you.

Fortunately, you already know how to raise your visibility, linked to your SME. You've seen it all over these pages. Now, just follow the same simple steps you learned earlier to create meaningful e-mail messages and rudimentary articles. Only this time play them out on a grander scale—on the Internet. Let's explore how you can rise up the ladder toward the top of the search engines.

One tactic—the one I illustrated with my little personal anecdote—is to get a substantial number of your articles posted (for free) on certain article-library web sites. I'll discuss this further in the section below.

But there are other, more basic ways. And they all work for small-sized practices, businesses, and organizations.

Technology caveat: Below I'll cover a menu of steps you can take yourself to raise your search rankings. In addition, various mumbo-jumbo techie things go on behind the curtains of your web site, which you and I never see and probably (unless you're way more computer savvy than me) don't understand, that also enter into the equation. Your web site guru can implant invisible codes and keywords that supposedly help get you ranked higher. These keywords are the ones that relate to topics that people search for (such as "retirement planning," "torn rotator cuff," "529 plans," and the like) and are not apparent to the naked eye on your site. This stuff used to be determinant in site ranking. That is no longer the case. The steps you'll see below matter much more now. However, this landscape keeps changing all the time. Make sure you have a conversation every few months with whomever runs your site to see if they are doing the latest and smartest things from their perspective. If they start using terms like *metatags*, smile and tell them to go on doing their thing for you. And then you go on following these strategies:

1. Get a grip on the right keywords. You need to know what words people type in when they want the info, and the service, you offer. It may not be what you

think—you're a practitioner, not a customer. If you're in the financial arena and are talking to a client about college savings, you may refer to "529 plans." But someone searching may type in "saving for college." So you need to identify all the right suspects. You can do this either by educated guesswork, asking your clients what they would do if searching, or you can buy the answers. Services like KeywordDiscovery.com and Wordtacker.com give you the lowdown for a reasonable fee. Google, last time I looked, does something similar for free. (I have not personally used these so I can't pass judgment on their effectiveness.)

2. Use the right keywords in the right places. You have to sprinkle them generously all over your site. And it can't just be done randomly, or tossed alone by themselves on an invisible little page that no one actually sees. Ignore any web techie who tells you this is OK. (Remember, web techies are just that—geniuses at creating and running sophisticated technology and software. Value them greatly for what they can do. But don't expect—or allow—them to be marketers, writers, business development consultants, or graphic artists too.) Use your keywords in proper context—in an article. But find a way to use them *often*: unlike on high school English compositions, repetition counts to the computerized searchers that scan your site and determine your ranking.

3. Above all, sprinkle those keywords all over the home page title, the headlines, and first paragraphs of all pages and articles.

4. Post lots of your articles and advice snippets on other organizations' web sites. By now, you (and anyone helping you write) are adept at cranking out five-tips-long articles, and little gems of wisdom weighing in at a mere two hundred to three hundred words, for your web site. This is good, but a little like singing in the

shower when you're Aretha Franklin. The people closest to you will be thrilled, but no one else gets to hear the magic. To attract clients and stimulate referrals, you've got to open the bathroom window and belt it out. In other words, extend your reach, to places where you'll be discovered by new people who haven't met you yet. You can do this by placing your articles on other sites. We'll cover how, and the main reason why, in the next section. But a secondary why is that you'll almost always get a link back to your site with each article you have posted somewhere else. And (can you guess what's coming?) those all-important search engines compulsively count how many links back to your site exist on the web. The more they find, the higher they rank you. Of course, you could always spend thousands of dollars on search engine advertising to get the same visibility, if you prefer. *And don't forget:* your articles should include the same keywords I just suggested sprinkling across your web site.

5. About those links back to your site: Have them point to new pages on your site (which your web guru can easily create) that have your SME *keywords* right in the web address. It turns out the search engines like this, too. If you're the town zookeeper with a thriving sideline training monkeys, you want those links to point visitors *not* to townzookeeper.com, but to monkeytrainer.townzookeeper.com.

6. Update your site often. This too will lift you in the search rankings, because Google and its brethren notice things like that. Every so often, throw a new item on, or update something already there. Just don't make it into a major project—it'll never get done if you do.

7. Don't put your keywords on your site in graphics files. If you use pdf files, catchy artwork, or even certain drop-down menus to display your keywords, the search engines will probably miss them. They read text files.

8. Think twice before switching your site to a new domain, or main web site address. The Googles of the world are pretty backlogged these days—they may not find you and rank you for weeks or months.

Lastly, don't go to the bank with any of these ideas. What works and what doesn't work on the web seems to be changing constantly. New strategies pop up frequently. Before fleshing out your Internet strategy, do some reading (by Googling a term like "search engine ranking") and get the up-to-date 411. Beware: it's entirely possible that the highest-ranked sites—because they are following strategies like these—can be three or four years old. Make sure the info you access is current.

Finding you while they're on other sites is the third way people get onto your site. Simply put, you need to be wherever your prospects are. The marketers who want you to buy a shiny new car this year don't sell by putting their advertising where they are—outside their assembly plants—but they go to where *you* are: on your favorite TV show, in the magazines you like to read. You're there for something else, but they lob a marketing message while you're there. In the same way—substituting meaty content for flashy advertising, of course—you have to put yourself where your prospects are. That's why you need to supplement the search engine-boosting strategies above by posting your articles on other organizations' web sites. That game works like this:

As you no doubt have noticed, there's a web site out there for every conceivable topic. The Internet, last time I looked, contained some fourteen billion pages.

Believe it or not, many of these sites actually want your tips and little articles. And they will publish them, at no cost to you. This is very good news, because with a little effort (which a staff person can do—and remember, your most junior employee is probably more adept at the Internet than you and me combined), you can identify some sites worth appearing on.

Whole books have been written on this topic, so I'll just stick to a few high points. The first type of site is the article library. The techies call these article directories. Basically they are large online repositories of articles written by experts—folks like you and me—on an endless number of subjects. Almost always, they are organized by topic. Many of these are open to the general public. But their primary purpose is to make large numbers of free articles available to various online publishers, mostly organizations and people who publish e-zines and e-newsletters. Without getting into the details, these online publishers need good material—they call it *content*—to fill their publications, so they pluck it from these one-stop-shopping libraries. If you are, say, a corporate time management expert, you want your articles to catch the eye of a publisher sifting through a library site for articles to fill the next issue of her newsletter on business productivity. That puts you right in front of an audience you want to reach—with a direct link back to *your* web site—courtesy of the library site.

Now, it turns out that your articles may also get picked up by other e-newsletter publishers whose audience does you no conceivable good. Your ingenious "Ten Tips to Care For Your Cactus Garden" article, for example, may somehow get carried in the "Northern Alaska Eskimo E-News" and you may not even know about it. This placement won't likely bring you business, but it is still a win. That's because your article will appear with an inbound link to your site—helping to lift your search rankings.

There are scads of article library sites out there. Some of them, through mysterious paths I can't fathom, even get picked up prominently by search portals like Google and Yahoo. Search under "article directories" and look for some that seem to fit your topic. Signing up as an author is generally free and painless. I have written for ezinearticles.com and BestManagementArticles.com with good results.

The library sites land you in front of your audience in a two-step process, and you don't control the outcome. A more direct route is to go right to the editors of the online publications that cater to your audience, and offer to be an author for them.

It's easy to identify these sites. They are known as niche sites—they serve specific slices of the market. Some of them are obvious. They are the official web sites of the organizations and associations that your target market belongs to. Others are simply web sites or publications that exist to reach and serve the same target market you want. There are all kinds of such sites, and they exist for the same reason—to make money in one way or another. Usually it's a way that has little to do with the articles themselves. The articles are there for the same reason radio stations carry popular music and football games—to draw in an audience that will notice the advertising that provides the revenue. Other web sites that can reach your audience, especially if your clientele is local, may be locally-based, such as the Blinkerville Computer Users Club or the Happytown Chamber of Commerce sites.

A word about these local web sites and local marketing: This especially makes sense if your business is overwhelmingly local. Being visible on them not only lifts your search rankings, it can actually bring you business. Someone in Phoenix searching for an accountant is likely to punch "accountant, Phoenix" into Google. To appear higher in the search results, if you're an accountant in Phoenix, use those two words in the headline and first sentence of as many of your articles as you can. This even makes sense to do in article library sites with their national focus. The more often your name appears next to your keyword and your geographic base, the better you will do as local residents shop online for experts. Doing this is actually easy and will not undermine our rule against being overly self-promotional. It's as simple as, "Phoenix Accountant Explains The 1040 Form." Or, let's consider the fictional case of Will Wipeout, an ex-surfing champ who is struggling to make a go of coaching young surfers in the town he just moved to. Will's article headline: "Oklahoma City Surfing Coach Urges Local Enthusiasts to Move to Malibu." His article's first sentence: "As a surfing trainer in Oklahoma City, I work with people who don't get to practice their sport very often."

I'm oversimplifying vastly, but the bottom line is this: you need to find yourself a few sites that will publish your articles. Search using your keywords—the same words that your clients would use—and using words relating to that audience. You'll find more sites than you'll know what to do with. This is a great task to assign a college intern, if you have one. He or she will have you posted on a half dozen sites before you get back from lunch.

The bottom line is to get yourself in front of the places your prospects already visit when they go online. This is the key to growth. In today's world, the power to reach audiences who don't yet know you—at infinitesimal cost—is unparalleled in human history. And it is getting easier, and cheaper, all the time.

I talked about blogs and podcasts in chapter 8. If you need a refresher, go back for a second look. Let's now look a little deeper into them. They are currently breaking out as a major web strategy.

With your *blog*, along with your own commentaries, you usually provide links to other web sites containing more resource information on the topic you're discussing. Why would you want to aid people in *leaving* your web site? Because, as we've seen, the more links between your web site and other web sites, the higher your ranking on Google and other search engines. So the more you send people *away* once they're done looking at you (they're about to leave anyway), the more you eventually draw people *to* you. Sound like a good tradeoff? It does to me. It's the marketing equivalent of when my beloved New York Mets trade a player who's about to become a free agent for a young prospect who'll blossom in a year or two.

Here's another way to tap into the power of blogs—without even creating your own. Read other people's blogs. Not the gossipy, snarky ones about celebrities or politics (save those for your leisure time) but the ones that are about, and for, your target audience. If your clients are professional engineers, keep a corner of your eye on blogs about engineering. Sure, you may not understand 99 percent of what they're talking about, and neither would I. But say you're a printer whose clientele is engineering firms. Sooner or later, you're going to spot a post by an engineer who complains about inferior document production. *Voila!* You have entrée to step in and post a thoughtful suggestion that will solve his problem (which you'll word skillfully to avoid being banished for selling your services blatantly), which is very likely to win you a new client or two. And fret not, you sure don't need to spend a lot of time reading engineers' blogs to make this strategy work. Once again, the techies have come through for us. They've invented something called a blog reader, which automatically scours cyberspace all day long for the topic we're interested in, and sends us a little summary of the best of what it captures.

Think of podcasts as the next logical step in the set of audio tools I covered earlier—CDs and audio files. The difference here is that, nice as they are, CDs are something you have to produce, then mail. Typically, people will pop them into the car CD player, or maybe into their computer or portable music disc player. Audio files eliminate the physical product, but now you have to either post them on your web site and wait for people to find them, or send them by e-mail and hope the recipient has time and ability to open them and listen.

With podcasts—and here too the technical part has become easy enough for us tech-illiterates to manage—you automatically send your recorded file (your words of wisdom reduced to an electronic blip that's the sound equivalent of a word-processed document) out to anyone who signs up to receive them from you on a regular basis. Through some electronic wizardry I couldn't begin to explain, these cool little sound bites of you can end up pretty much automatically in your recipient's iPod, where he or she can listen to it in the supermarket or on the train, with minimal hassle on everyone's part. Imagine—you're on the air somewhere, for someone, all the time.

And that's the ABCs of expertise marketing on the Internet. One thing I can guarantee: it will have changed by the time you read this.

> *Keep up with the changes. I regularly update a list of good online resources and vendors I come across to help with the strategies in this chapter. That includes help for e-newsletters, search-engine rankings, blog writing and reading, and whatever else is new. See my web site,* **www.MediaImpact.biz/resources/online.**

11

THE BEST WAY TO GET PUBLICITY: DATE A CELEBRITY. HERE'S THE SECOND BEST WAY

There's so much to cover on publicity that I could write a book about this topic alone. (Oh, wait... I did: *102 Publicity Tips to Grow A Business or Practice*, available at Amazon.com).

If you get one thing from this chapter, make it this: **Press releases are almost useless for getting publicity. There are much better, and easier, tactics.** *Read this chapter carefully if you want to learn how the game really works.*

Getting publicity in the media, for free, is a lot like everything else I've referenced in this book.

People in the professions think they can't possibly do it without expensive help or special expertise. They think that even with help, they probably won't succeed unless they work for a big, household name organization. Yet they suspect it can help grow their practice or business.

Wrong, wrong, and right.

For a smart subject matter expert like you, publicity isn't as hard to obtain as it may seem. It's a lot like asking someone on a date when you're fourteen, or (I suspect) like diving: thinking you can't do it is half of what makes it hard.

But you've just absorbed ten chapters' worth of learning how you're an expert with knowledge that prospects need and value, and that if you make a modest effort to get it in their hands, they will respond favorably.

With publicity, substitute "media" for "prospect"—and not much else changes. Here's why:

To a great extent, the media are driven by the need for experts who can explain what's happening in this great big, rapidly changing, complex world of ours.

Hey, that means you and me!

You, as a subject matter expert, are often in demand with the media. They need you to interpret and explain what's happening. And, because you know more about your field than they do, you know what's happening *next*, which means you can suggest story ideas to the media, with the reasonable expectation that you'll usually be quoted or featured in those stories.

Remember this: reporters are experts in their job, not in your professional field. Even the most astute legal affairs reporter, for instance, is unlikely to know anywhere near as much about developments in the field as most any lawyer. And 99.99 percent of reporters are generalists in the extreme: not only are they not experts in your field, they may barely know anything about it— because their job is not to know, but to find the people who do know, and then explain it in simple terms to everyone else.

And that's how you come to be a valuable resource to them. After all my years in media and PR, I know this to be one of the ten basic rules of the game: You don't have to be the smartest, the biggest, the most credentialed in your profession, or an employee of the largest firm.

You just have to know *enough* about your business, and you have to be in the right place at the right time.

Getting publicity is all about putting yourself out there.

To start getting free publicity, to put yourself in a position to receive, you have to understand the basics of how the media game works. Here's the crash course. (Or, if you prefer, skip it and pay a PR agency several thousand dollars a month to do it for you.)

Let's start by reviewing *why* you want publicity (aside from your oversized ego, the way it impresses dates, and the happy smile it plants on your mother's face.) Publicity gets your name and expertise in front of people who don't know you yet; it widens your funnel of leads. It does this much more cost-effectively than anything else. And it gives you credibility you literally can't buy *("Hey, this consultant sounds like she really knows her stuff—and the* Bugle *is quoting her as an expert!")*.

There are basically three types of stories that will get you smiling along with Mom. The first is the article you write yourself. In the biz, it's called a *byliner* because it carries your byline. It's basically the kind of article I've discussed in earlier chapters, dressed up and expanded to maybe five to six hundred words. In a byliner, you hold forth on a particular topic and either offer valuable insights, information, or an informed point of view (though if you're smart, you'll stay far away from anything that looks or smells like politics.) As you've seen, these articles are prevalent on the Internet. They also appear often in your town's local papers, and in the professional/industrial (or "trade") press that serves your target market. (Helpful note: Getting published in an accounting journal is nice if you're an accountant, but unlikely to bring you any business. An accountant who serves the retail food industry would be much better off getting published in *Supermarket Monthly News*—not a real publication, one I made up to illustrate my point.) These publications have very limited opportunities for people like you and me to submit articles to. That's because their pages are largely filled with news articles written by staff people. But they typically do have guest column spots. To score here, you need to first learn which publications matter most to your clients (that's easy; you ask them or notice what's lying around their reception area).

Then you, or someone on your staff, checks superficially into that publication (either the printed or online version) to find those guest column spots. You eyeball a few issues to get a sense of who's writing, what topics and approaches they follow, and the style the publication seems to favor. You write the *entire* article first and submit it, following the submission guidelines that generally appear in the publication or its web site. You make sure your article links *your* expertise to *their* interests, as in, "Ten Tax Tips To Lift Supermarket Profits." It rarely pays to bother with one of those open-ended, "Would you like an article on the ten best hooks and lures to catch a trout?" query letters. The answer is almost always some variation of "Maybe." When your byliner is accepted, make sure—just as in Internet articles—that it includes a blurb about your expertise and, if the publication will consent, a link to your web site with an offer. You'll usually hear within a few weeks if it's been accepted. If it hasn't been, just find another outlet—print or online—to send it to. (And if all else fails, publish it yourself and mail or e-mail it to your mailing list.)

The second type of good story is the big-splash, two-page glossy feature on you, your entire organization, and why it's great. This is the Holy Grail of media; in the biz it's known simply as the "home run." This is the kind of article most people envision and dream of when they think publicity. It's also the hardest and rarest to get. Pinning all your hopes on it is a little like thinking baseball consists only of home runs, or that the only baskets that count in basketball are slam dunks and buzzer-beating three pointers. The profile spread is similarly dramatic, yet not the only way to score. I urge most small and mid-sized businesses not to build a strategy around achieving this as their primary goal. It can be done, but it takes a long time unless you get really lucky, and in the interim you usually miss out on other good opportunities. Big-splash features usually happen naturally on their own, as an eventual outcome of following a PR strategy with less lofty initial goals. Sort of how squirreling your frequent-flyer points gets you on a plane to Hawaii for free, if you are patient and don't obsess over looking for ways to get there tomorrow.

The third type of story is the kind you can get yourself into—and often. It's the type where the media are reporting on some news development, or explaining some important trend or issue, in your field of expertise. In their story, they'll need to quote the experts who can explain succinctly to a general audience what it all means. *You* can be that expert—acting as that resource I discussed at the top of this chapter. This is the type of story I urge professionals and smaller organizations to pursue most aggressively, because you can do it yourself.

Really.

In the beginning you may only be quoted for a sentence or two (which isn't bad in itself, when you consider how most of your competitors don't even get that). But pretty soon, as you build a relationship or two and practice the basic techniques, you'll be quoted more extensively, maybe even with your photo included. So, instead of being intimidated at the very thought of contacting a reporter (as in "*I wouldn't know how to start to approach the media,*" or "*Why would they talk to me? I'm nobody special*" or "*I don't know anybody there*"), let's examine calmly and logically, like the professionals we are, how to make publicity happen. Let's uncover a couple insights into how reporters think, and how their job works.

As you've seen, a reporter's job nearly every day is to find some expert who can be quoted in the article they are writing. Every time they show up for work, it's an opportunity for you to get publicity! But the reporter who doesn't know you yet is like the prospect you haven't met: much as they could benefit from your wisdom, you need to do something to start the relationship.

Think of the personal, or romantic, relationships in your life, and how they started. Sometimes you just connected and hit it off instantly: "*Hey, why don't we go for some coffee right now?*" Sometimes, you kept trying and trying to win the other person's attention: days and days of small talk, eventually you sent a card or note, plus a fair share of flirting, before you finally broke through.

Surprise—media folks are people too, and starting a relationship is no different. Do not be concerned with whether it happens instantly or over time. Just work on making it happen.

In the end, it comes down to three routes:

Route #1: You're aware of a good potential news story—one the publication you want to be in hasn't thought to write yet. This happens all the time, because you're in your profession every day, often closer to new trends and developments than they are. How often have you seen something on your topic in the paper and thought, "Hey, that's old news"? You may know of a recent court decision, or a law taking effect, that is going to significantly impact many people in your target market. Or it may just be some new trend that all the practitioners have been seeing lately. Whatever and whenever it is, what you need to do is so elementary that it astounds me why everyone doesn't do it.

You just tell a reporter about it.

You've prepared for this by keeping an eye on the publication you want to be in. You know the name of the reporter who most frequently writes about your topic. If it's a small publication, you know the name of the editor. You've quietly gotten the names, e-mail addresses, and phone numbers of these people, whom I'll call the "likeliest suspects" in your quest for publicity.

When the moment comes, you'll just send them a **very short** e-mail or call them with a brief phone message: *"Hi, I hope I'm catching you at a good time… I'm a local expert on taxes and there's something you may want to know."* You then tell them in two or three sentences—**only**—the high points and the big picture—how it affects their audience—**only**. Your job now is not to teach the reporter everything. It's to sell the story idea. Then you wait for the call back. Sometimes it doesn't come. Or you'll get a snide, "Whadda you know about a story, mister?" Or—the worst—you might even see your idea in print a week later, with no mention of you.

But as often as not, you will get a reply from a curious reporter. When that happens, you shift deftly from your previous sales mode to the resource mode. You're there to help the reporter; you have no other ulterior motive (though, of course you do!). Answer the questions and stick to the facts. This is *not* the time to sell yourself. If the reporter agrees it's a story, you'll probably be quoted as the expert who can explain and interpret it to the masses. You're on your way to media stardom, because if you answer fully, speak intelligently, and return their calls **promptly** (this single act means more to the press than all your degrees and credentials combined), they'll probably call you next time something comes up.

Route #2: This time, you know they *have* to do a story on your topic. Two weekend sailors just collided their boats in the harbor, and there are serious injuries and property damage. The press is all over the story, and you're an expert on maritime torts. They need to quote someone about the broad general issues at stake (of course you can't comment on the specifics of this incident and they know that); it might as well be you. Again, you just reach out informally to the publication as I just discussed. Why *wouldn't* they include you? (This tactic works best the same day the event happens—you'll learn of it on the radio or the noon TV news, and call the newspaper or maybe the evening news right away. But on a big story that lives for two days, you can also call on the second day.)

Route # 3: The publicity gods have given us all this way to use in the 80 percent of the time when no obvious, immediate news story looms, as in Routes #1 and #2. We're blessed to have it; otherwise we'd all spend a lot of time just waiting around for the right opportunity. Route # 3 is to find clever, non-intrusive ways to build media relationships when not much else is going on. The reporters or publications you're after will listen just as well—if not better—when it's clear you are *not* trying to elbow your way into tomorrow's story. Way # 3 is like that personal romantic relationship you once started by being so creative and persistent. Remember how you'd concoct any conceivable way to strike up a conversation with the person to whom you were attracted? Remember how challenging this may have felt? Remember how (maybe) you finally broke through on the fourth or fifth try? Same situation here. You're like the insecure high-schooler with an eye on the football captain: you want the media's attention, yet they're dating a different cheerleader every night. Don't give up!

Here's how it works:

You'll get their attention first by e-mailing or calling them about something that's visibly non-urgent for you. Perhaps you've read their latest story on some topic that you're familiar with and—as is almost the case—you notice something they got not quite right, or that they omitted because they didn't know about. That's your cue to e-mail a (diplomatically-worded) informative message that positions you firmly as their friend and resource:

"Tony, loved your story on the trout fever that's killing the fish in our local harbor. Did you know that they had that problem upstate too, and they figured out a solution?"

Or, "Amanda, your story on this year's corn crop was really informative. Have you heard about the big meeting the farmers are holding next month to consider cloning their seeds for the first time in history?" You're not asking anything from them, you're just sending the unspoken signal that you're informed, and willing to help them. When they realize that (and they will) you'll move to the top of their list next time they need to quote an expert.

Bonus way to reach the media: volunteer to be a media resource for the local chapter of your professional association. When those reporters need to dig into that trout fever story, they'll often call the nearest chapter of the Fisherman's Association or the Fish Doctor's Association. Half the time, those groups will pull out their list of members who have volunteered to be available to the media. *Get yourself on that list.* I have had clients with thick stacks of press clippings from following this simple tactic alone.

By the way, everything I discussed earlier in the marketing chapters, about slicing your subject matter expertise to highly specific single-focus bits of information, applies doubly with the media. "Everything you ever wanted to know about molecular biology" will never be a news story. "New scientific research suggests ten steps to reduce cancer risk" will always be a story. (And the research doesn't have to be yours, either. If someone else's big study in your field breaks into the general news, and you can explain what it all means to the average Joe and Jen, you're ready for your close-up.)

Here's all that most media folks care about:

"Is it news?" (i.e., is it something new?) "Is it important?" (Does it affect their audience?) "Is it interesting?" (Will their audience want to pay attention to it?)

And last but not least, "Will I score points with my editor by doing this story?"

Just don't forget that when it *is* a story, it's a story *today*. Don't wait until next month to check in with a reporter because your schedule looks lighter then. It's ancient history to the media at that point. My good friend Chuc Barnes, a truly wise expert on time management and delivering effective presentations, got "The Call" just as he was starting his business. The Call, in the media game, is the one from Oprah. The one that invites you to be on her show. "I'm too busy starting up," Chuc thought. "I'll tell them I can do this in a few weeks." A business associate quickly suggested to Chuc that he might want to rethink his position. But by the time Chuc called back, it was too late. Oprah's bookers had simply gone on to the next expert they could find. It's what bookers always do. They are in a hurry. (Chuc is so talented that he has gone on to great success nonetheless, I am happy to report.)

Call reporters and bookers back promptly. I once heard a tale—perhaps apocryphal, perhaps not—of a surgeon who'd leave the operating room to field a good media call. That may be extreme, and if I knew who this doctor was, I'd pass the name along so you could avoid him or her. But if you're not a brain surgeon, I do suggest you drop virtually anything else on your agenda should the right media opportunity come along. It won't stay dangling in your grasp for very long.

SERVING THE MEDIA

 Being a resource for the media is "my primary way" of attracting new business, says Coon Rapids, Minnesota, certified financial planner Greg Zandlo. He's been quoted almost anywhere important you can think of. And, every time he is, new prospects call. "In this day and age, what has worked tremendously is to build rapport with all the media sources—magazines, newspapers, journals."

When a time-pressed reporter calls on deadline, Greg makes sure he's quick and thorough in helping out. A media inquiry "receives the highest priority [and] immediate attention." If the inquiry topic does not match his areas of expertise, he'll refer the reporter to another financial planner.

Attaining publicity "reinforces that I have the kind of third-party credibility that prospects like to see," he explains.

Greg hires no agency or publicist. He just devotes an hour or two a week to getting publicity—either talking to reporters or, if none calls that week, "brainstorm about current industry hot buttons that a media source could write about…then contact them."

"What I don't do," he adds, "is create a large media kit, glossy photo, reams of past quotes, etc. I think it is totally unprofessional, let alone self-absorbing. The media's time is as valuable as mine."

"I guess you could call it demand pull PR, rather than push PR."

To leverage the publicity he gets for his business, North East Asset Management, Greg sends copies of articles he's in to his prospects. The underlying message: "This is the kind of work you can expect from me."

When you approach the media in the manner I've been discussing—humbly as a resource, from a mindset of existing to help them—they tend to respond. When you approach them from a mindset of selling yourself, of trying to push them into quoting you, it can also work sometimes. But you have to be the loudest, brashest, most persistent, and aggressive, to break through. As Donald Trump is, and does. As in the Little Leaguers in that story about my minivan back in chapter 1. If that's you, you're probably a budding media star. If it's not you, I find the "resource" approach works more often for more people.

To return to the dating analogy, talking to the media is not unlike approaching someone you'd like to go out with. Sure, you may be a little nervous or even intimidated. But as long as you remember that the person on the other side of the conversation is a regular person just like you, and as long as you act naturally instead of coming off as a jerk in some forced, artificial manner, your odds are good.

Now let's tackle The Myth of the Press Release. Most people think this is the tool of choice for getting the media's attention.

The reality: the average reporter receives four or more press releases an hour. I don't know too many reporters who write four stories a day, much less an hour. Guess where all those extra press releases end up?

Another reporter recently told a forum he receives about three hundred emails containing story suggestions, or pitches, a day.

Press releases are for news. Real news. Significant news. Most of us don't make big news in our businesses or practices (and that's probably fine. To the media, real news is when someone goes wacko in your lobby with a submachine gun.)

If you produce or sell a product, launching it with a press release makes sense. If you're speaking next month at the library and the public is invited, that's a press release too. Otherwise, consider the ten-to-1 rule: do one press release for every ten of the more informal, personal kinds of contacts I've described in this chapter.

The next-to-last thing you need to know about publicity is the power of the first words, the first line. Even more than with your e-mail, it's critical to nail the essence, importance, and urgency of your message in the subject line, the headline, and the first sentence. Work, work, work on this one skill, and your media results will likely soar. Ask someone you trust for feedback, then go back and edit, re-edit, and re-edit. A top comedian, Jerry Seinfeld I believe, once recounted spending hours on trimming a ten-word one-liner down to four words. That's the idea.

The last big thing to know about publicity is the importance and power of leveraging it.

Everything you do in your publicity should connect to, build on, and enhance everything else you do. All the components are interrelated.

If you're giving a public speech, as you just learned, you can do a press release in advance to build up the advance word to lift attendance. Then, after the speech, you can boil your remarks down to ten-tips size and send that off to the media as an article.

When they publish it, you post it on your web site, and e-mail copies to your database. You print reprints, and mail them out.

When the Dental Hygienists Association invites you to write an article for their newsletter, because their members are your target audience, you'll change a few minor points and send it off to the Medical Technicians Association newsletter, because they're your market too.

Everything is interrelated. Everything has more than one use. When you act this way, two good things happen: you get more mileage and impact out of each action…. And you're more apt to take more actions, because you know the payoff will be greater each time.

12

BUILD AND SUSTAIN MOMENTUM

For me, taking my car to the dealership for routine maintenance yields a clear advantage: They take the thinking out of it for me. Between the manufacturer and the dealership, they've come up with a handy-dandy little grid chart—one that's understandable even to the likes of me. Plainly and visually, it shows me how often the various maintenance procedures need to be performed, and precisely what needs to happen every three, six, twelve, and twenty-four months. I no longer have to be a semi-expert on the subject. No more reading manuals or anything else.

In that spirit, this chapter is for people who feel about marketing their practice the way I feel about maintaining my car: just tell me what to do, and when to do it, and skip all the details. So, here's what a typical year of **mPOWER system expertise marketing** might look like:

JANUARY

- Redo your e-mail signature to add a "benefits of working with me" phrase.
- Write a one-screen-long, five bullet-point e-mail message: "Five Things You Need to Know or Do This

Year" that fits your clients' current concerns. Send it to your list of prospects and sustainers (key referral providers).

FEBRUARY

- Contact a local organization or association whose members are your target market, and offer to speak there for free.
- Send a helpful, informational one-page fax message about something new or important to the people on your list.

MARCH

- Launch your short-but-sweet e-newsletter, using one of the simple, do-it-yourself e-mail services mentioned earlier to take 90 percent of the work and inconvenience out of the job.

APRIL

- Post something new, useful, and informational on your web site.
- Send your prospect list a link to it by e-mail.

MAY

- Do another one-page item of tips and advice. This time, print it and send it by regular mail.

JUNE

- Create and send your e-newsletter.

JULY

- Write a brief informational article for another organization's web site—one that reaches your target market.
- When it's posted, e-mail your list a heads-up and a link to it.

AUGUST

- Send your list an expertise-marketing postcard.

SEPTEMBER

- Create and send an e-newsletter.

OCTOBER

- Give the speech you booked back in February.
- Three weeks before it, alert your mailing list by e-mail about it, and send a one-page press release to the media.
- Right after it, jot down the highlights of your remarks. Post them on your web site and send them to the media.

NOVEMBER

- Send another marketing postcard to your list.

DECEMBER

- Send the year's fourth e-newsletter.
- Add a warm, personal touch to your holiday cards to your best clients, prospects, and sustainers.

To get a printable version of this calendar and the action agenda that follows, go to www.MediaImpact.biz/resources/calendar.

APPENDIX

THE mPOWER CHECKLIST: 25 THINGS TO DO NOW

1. Rewrite your biography to include language that talks about how you benefit your clients, and what you've accomplished. Remove half of what's in there now about your credentials and the titles of all the jobs you've ever held.

2. Change your voicemail greeting to add a brief phrase that relates to the work you do with clients.

3. Spend an hour in a quiet place thinking about, and writing down, the benefits that clients get when they work with you. Keep distilling and refining what you've written to be more and more concrete and specific.

4. Spend another hour, on another day, thinking about who your target market is. Do you know? Do you need to refine your target group?

5. Compile or update a good database of the prospects, clients, and sustainers (referral providers) in that

market. Make sure it includes e-mail addresses, phone numbers, and mailing addresses.

6. Change your e-mail signature to add a brief phrase that relates to the work you do with clients.

7. Check out Constant Contact, Topica, or one of the other services that make it a snap to create your own, attractive e-newsletter as often as you want to.

8. Send your prospects and clients an e-newsletter telling them in five sentences or bullets—one per item—five things they should do now.

9. If your sustainers are in a different market segment than your clients (i.e., you serve homebuyers but get business from realtors) create another five-things e-newsletter just for them.

10. Write (or rewrite) your basic one-minute "elevator speech" that you use to describe and market yourself, to focus on the benefits you bring to clients, and to remove any self-promotional hype.

11. Make up a new business card. Add a phrase like the one for Step # 6.

12. Sit down in a quiet place and ask yourself, "If I could be interviewed and quoted in the media on one current topic in my field this year, what would it be?"

13. Follow the tips in the publicity chapter of this book to make that interview happen.

14. Reserve some personal retreat time away from the office on a regular basis—say one Monday morning or one Friday afternoon a month. Go to a local Starbucks, hotel lounge, airport club, or business center—wherever you can escape from the daily fray. Use that time to tackle the challenges and long-term issues you can't get to in your busy office.

15. Check out one of the new, low-cost Internet-based document/data backup systems for your computer, and sign up for regular automatic updates. Even if you already have a backup device.

16. Complete the following sentence: "It's (whatever the month is). What's happening in the next thirty days that my clients need to know about and act on?"

17. Write five lines based on the above, and mail it to them.

18. Repeat the same process as in Step #16, only make it sixty days.

19. Send an e-mail or make a call to a reporter suggesting they do a story on what you came up with in Step #18.

20. Send your list an expertise marketing piece by fax.

21. Take the single most important thing your clients need to know this year, write exactly one sentence summarizing it, and put it on a postcard as another expertise marketing piece.

22. Take fifteen minutes to ask yourself, "Instead of just thinking about how to make my web site better, how could I make people want to come back to it more often?"

23. Cancel your plans and your budget for a splashy brochure and put the money instead into augmenting your site with some of the ideas you just thought of.

24. Add your web site address to all your materials—business cards, stationery, marketing pieces.

25. Share your best successes and marketing ideas with me at info@MediaImpact.biz.

CHECKLIST FOR AN ACTION AGENDA

Get a printable copy at
www.MediaImpact.biz/resources/calendar

My market is: _____

My strategies are: _____

_____

_____

My subject matter expertise is: _____

My message to the market is: _____

My goals for the next thirty days are _____
and _____ .

My action steps to reach my goals are:

_____

_____

_____

_____

POSTSCRIPT:
YES, YOU WILL

You can change the way you think about marketing, the way you do marketing, and the results you get from it.

You really can. And in so doing, you can transform your business—and what you get out of it.

All it takes to start is to realize that for the professional services, marketing isn't what someone told you it was. To understand that selling your services is really just showing others the value of working with you and finding the right "others" who need what you do. And that the best way for you to accomplish that is ... to simply be yourself. And to communicate who you are, and how others have found that to be valuable, in a straightforward way. To be always useful and informative when going to the marketplace, never pushy, intrusive, and self-promotional.

You can do this, I promise. And when you do, I want to hear about how you did it, and what worked best for you. Send me your story. I'll publish the best of them—in the next edition of this book, in my other published materials, or on my web site.

You can reach me at info@MediaImpact.biz. I can't wait to hear about what you've accomplished.

WANT TO LEARN MORE?

Ned Steele speaks about marketing and growing a professional practice to business audiences (professional conferences and meetings, association programs, seminars, and individual companies and organizations).

Ned also works one-on-one with professional practices, entrepreneurs, and nonprofit organizations that want to build their organization and accelerate growth.

A former newspaperman (*New York Post, New York Daily News*) and public relations firm executive and owner, Ned is also the author of *102 Publicity Tips To Grow A Business Or Practice.*

Here's how to reach Ned:
(212) 243-8383
info@ MediaImpact.biz
www.MediaImpact.biz

To order more books:
Online: www.MediaImpact.biz
E-mail: info@MediaImpact.biz
or at Amazon.com

For group and bulk purchases, special rates are available.
Please contact info@MediaImpact.biz.